The Afflicted Path

KMoryn

The Afflicted Path

The Pain

Kori Moryn White

Dedication

To my son Kingston Niles Velez,

You are my light, my purpose, and my second chance. Before you, I was lost—stumbling down a path that led only to darkness. But the moment I knew I was with child, everything shifted. You became my reason to fight, to grow, and to heal.

Because of you, I chose a different road—one paved with love, resilience, and hope. Every step I take now is guided by the promise I made to you: to give you the life I once dreamed of, to fill your world with the love, joy, and opportunities I missed along the way.

Thank you for saving me in ways I didn't know I needed saving. You are my greatest teacher, my proudest achievement, and the love of my life.

This book is for you, Mama Son. May you always know how deeply you are loved.

With all my heart,

Mom

Table of Contents:

Introduction

KMoryn

Affliction refers to something that causes pain or suffering. Psalm 119:71 says, "It is good for me that I was afflicted, that I may learn Your statutes." This verse suggests that affliction can be a powerful tool to motivate us to learn and align with God's ways. While we live in the flesh and possess free will, our choices unfold within the framework of a story already written by God.

Thirty-seven years into my story, I have faced many afflictions. My childhood was filled with adverse experiences, so I witnessed the good, the bad, and everything in between. I took what was meaningful to me and vowed to be the opposite of what I would not say I liked growing up.

The central theme of my life's story is trauma. I found myself in circumstances beyond my control from the moment I was born. Existing placed me in a position that would lead to challenges and difficulties as the years passed.

Our first experience of true love should ideally come from our parents, followed by the loyalty and love of our siblings. However, this is not always the reality. In my story, many of life's hardest lessons came from my mother and sisters. They were the first to teach me about heartbreak, disloyalty, dysfunction, and even hatred. They became the source of many of life's hardest lessons.

Most of my life has been spent overcoming various afflictions. There were moments when life seemed to be going smoothly, yet even then, I was still in the process of healing from something I was determined not to let defeat me. Along the way, I forgave the unforgivable, held on longer than I should have, and invested myself in things and people that did not serve me. Deep down, I always believed there was something better meant for me, even though I struggled to understand why I had to endure so much pain.

Reflecting on my life and revisiting my earliest memories has revealed how far I have come and the generational curses I have been able to break. My struggles and afflictions have shaped me into a stronger, wiser, and better person. While I may not be rich in material wealth, my true riches lie in my morals, values, and the love I carry in my heart.

Through it all, I have learned to be grateful for the afflictions I have endured. Every hard lesson eventually revealed its purpose. As you read my story, you will witness the growth and transformation of KMoryn—a journey shaped by pain, resilience, and, ultimately, gratitude.

Chapter I

Meet the Family

Picture this: Sicily, 1922. Just kidding, that is a classic line from The Golden Girls, a show that aired long before my time. Still, it is one of those phrases that, like a favorite song, can transport you back to a specific moment. Hearing it brings back memories of sitting on the living room floor with toys scattered around while 'The Golden Girls played softly in the background. The comforting aroma of something homemade drifted from the kitchen, wrapping me in a sense of peace. In those moments, life felt simple, and innocence served as a shield against the complexities of the outside world. We cherish these memories as reminders of when life felt safe and simple.

In the summer of 1987, the world changed when God blessed it with one of His most beautiful creations: me, Kori Moryn White. I am the fourth of five children, born in Los Angeles, California. My brother Brian is the oldest, followed by Michelle, Amber, then myself, and finally my youngest brother Jaxon. My mother, Janet, married Brian's father for ten years before they divorced because of her unfaithful dealings with Michelle and Amber's father. I have a dad, and Jaxon also has his father.

My mother was a force to be reckoned with. Tall and slim, with hair cascading down her back, she exuded fierce intelligence and undeniable charisma. She was unstoppable—graduating high school early, publishing her first short story at eighteen, and wielding a vocabulary that could leave anyone in awe. Growing up under the strict rule of her military father, she knew discipline and order well, but as soon as she gained her freedom, she lived wildly, like a preacher's kid who finally broke free.

I did not spend much time with my oldest brother, Brian, because of our age difference; he is 20 years older than me. Brian got into trouble and was sentenced to three life sentences when I was only two years old. Our bond and relationship started growing once I was old enough to converse over the phone. Brian always talked about how he had the best version of our mother: young, vibrant, in love, and at the peak of her career.

When my mother's relationship with Brian's father started to falter, Brian asked to live with our grandmother, whom I called Gma. From the age of nine onward, she essentially raised him. Michelle and Amber were born after my mother and Brian's father separated. I do not remember hearing much about my mother's life with their father, but I do know that during this period, she was deeply involved in drugs.

During the nineties, the war on drugs in Los Angeles was at its peak. It was Michelle and Amber's father who introduced my mother to drugs and street life. Rumor had it that Brian's aunt was married to one of L.A.'s top drug dealers, while Michelle and Amber's father worked as a runner or something similar at a lower level. One day, my mother accompanied Brian's aunt to a meeting with my sister's father for some quick business. At that moment, my mother was overwhelmed with an intense feeling of lust.

This man played a key role in derailing my mother's life. After introducing her to his dangerous lifestyle, she began to spiral. After her divorce, everything she had received in the settlement gradually slipped away.

I came four years after Amber. My mother and father knew each other because their mothers were best friends. They tried the romantic thing, but it did not last. Jaxon is only 17 months younger than me. His father was a sweet and gentle man who was around the longest. Their relationship was unique. He never lived with us because he was married, but his wife was fully aware of the relationship he and my mother had. Jaxon has a sister of his age who always comes over with their father for play dates.

My family tree is not huge. I have four siblings but no aunts, uncles, or cousins since both of my parents are the only children. I do have a second and third-generation family through my Gma's siblings, but like most only children, friends became family, so I grew up with an extended family that blood could not make any closer. Despite having a small family, one would think we would all be close-knit. In my family, that statement is far from the truth. I believe my story will reveal how that came to be.

In 1991, when I was four years old, I lived with my mother, two sisters, and younger brother in a ghetto neighborhood in Los Angeles. I do not remember many details, just vague flashes of an empty apartment with a small table lamp on the floor and a single mattress against the wall in the bedroom that we all piled into. Outside was a tan first-level apartment with dirt pathways. My earliest memories are tied to an incident and a taste. I remember trying to jump over a small, shade-less lamp on the floor. I am not sure what I was wearing exactly; it could have been a shirt or a dress, but I know I only had undies on my bottom half. As I jumped, the light blinded me, and I landed on the hot bulb, burning my inner thigh. Later that day, my burn turned into a pocket of pus, and I had to walk funny until it burst down my leg. At that age, I also remember my mother giving us a teaspoon of cod liver oil to keep us from getting sick. It was the thickest, most awful-tasting, slowest-to-swallow, and most disgusting thing I had ever experienced. That taste is forever etched in my memory.

Gma, God rest her soul. I have only known my grandmother as a God-fearing, prayerful warrior. I knew her as a straightforward, no-nonsense woman who said exactly what was on her mind. However, I have heard she led a highly active life in her younger years. She was the second of twelve children, nine of whom were boys. At just 14 years old, she gave birth to my mother. However, my mother and Gma were raised more like sisters with many other children. I remember my mother saying that, as a child, she thought Gma favored her as a little sister because she always gave her extra care compared to the other siblings. My mother discovered Gma's identity one day during an argument. My mother and Gma were going back and forth, and Gma's sister yelled out, "Stop talking to your mother like that." At that moment, the cat was out of the bag, and my mother learned her sister was actually her mother. My mother was maybe five or six then, and I'm sure it was all very confusing to her. It was not until Gma became an adult and married that she and her husband began raising my mother as their child.

My Gma was built Ford Tough. She ran the streets and went upside a couple of heads in her day.

Eventually, she turned her life over to God and lived righteously. By the time I was born, my Gma was divorced and married to God. My grandmother was a constant presence in our lives. Between 1992 and 1993, she realized how deeply my mother had been consumed by a life on the streets. Drugs had taken control of her, leading to the loss of her job, and leaving her unable to provide for us. She did her best, but life had swallowed her whole. My grandmother, who had just retired and lived in a one-bedroom senior citizen apartment, took in my siblings and me. I was five years old at the time. I remember the smell of her hot water cornbread. I would not say I liked it then, but now I would love to dip a piece in some collard green juice, and yams.

Before living with my grandmother, I had no memory of my day-to-day life because I was too young to remember. Michelle, 14, and Amber, 9, have memories about which I have only heard. Living with Gma marks the start of my earliest memories. She made sure we were all enrolled in school, and for me, it was my very first time attending. Michelle was already in high school, while Amber, Jaxon, and I attended Manchester Elementary School. I was in kindergarten. I remember waking up every morning before the sun rose to wash our faces and brush our teeth. Then, we had put on our neatly pressed school uniforms that Gma had ironed on Sunday after church, preparing for the week. Grandma had everything laid out: our backpacks were always by the front door, and as we headed out, she handed us our cafeteria tickets—blue for breakfast and red for lunch while making sure our faces were freshly coated with Vaseline. The biggest stress of my day was making sure I did not lose those tickets, as they determined how we ate during the first half of the day. Thankfully, Gma always had dinner waiting on the stove.

Every day after school, we had to practice reading not a schoolbook or nursery rhyme but from the Bible. I remember sitting at the table when Amber asked, "Why do we have to read this? People don't even talk like 'thee' and 'thy.'" Before she could finish, Gma had already knocked her to the ground. Gma was a bit extra with discipline; everything was considered talking back. Words like "dumb," "shut up," and any back-and-forth definitely got your mouth rinsed out with soap. Gma was an old school, born in 1950. We never missed church on

Sundays. Grandma made sure we sat with our backs straight and our hands in our laps—no fidgeting, no slouching, and no dozing off if we valued our safety. That little pinch and twist she would give was enough to keep us in line.

I do not think we stayed with Gma long before it became too much for her to handle. Michelle had started skipping school, Amber had her challenges, and Jaxon and I were like having a pair of young twins to care for. Grandma went from a full income multiple times a month, to a fixed once a month, from feeding herself to providing for five mouths. On top of that, she had to make sure we all had clothes and shoes. Although Brian was already in prison, she took on the responsibility of sending him care packages and money for his commissary. My last memory of living with my grandmother was the night I had chickenpox. She bathed me in oatmeal to help soothe and dry out my skin.

I dropped oatmeal everywhere, so she made me go to bed early. I was in the living room on a rollaway fold-out bed. That night, the 1994 Northridge Earthquake tore Los Angeles up. The apartment was shaking, the china in the armoire was flying, the cabinets were swinging, and dishes were breaking. We all took cover in Gma's room, where she had everything, we needed to survive: a case of water, flashlights, extra batteries, a military-style packet of food, and several first aid kits. Before needing all this, we constantly made jokes about the stuff on the side of her bed. Who knew it would all come in handy one night? The next morning, when daylight broke and we entered the living room, everything was ruined. My grandmother suffered a significant loss that day. It was not long after that she made the difficult decision to turn us over to the state, and we were all placed in foster care.

Chapter II

John and Rita Wright

Before living with my grandmother, my life was defined by poverty. We often had no electricity, no gas, no food, and sometimes no adult supervision while my mother was out on the streets using drugs. Our only light came from an extension cord borrowed from a neighbor's apartment. By law, our living conditions were grounds for removal from the home. We were victims of parents with substance abuse issues. Although I was there, I was not old enough to comprehend or identify what was lacking. Michelle and Amber were both old enough to be profoundly affected by this experience, planting a seed in them that would follow them for the rest of their lives.

In 1853, a minister and social reformer, Charles Brace, founded The Children's Aid Society and initiated the "Orphan Train" movement. His mission was to relocate orphaned and homeless children from overcrowded Eastern cities to foster homes in the Midwest. Over time, this concept evolved, laying the foundation for the more structured and government-supported foster care systems in the United States. By the early 20th century, states began developing child welfare agencies and passing laws to protect children's welfare. Those who become foster parents commit themselves to providing basic needs such as adequate food, clothing, and shelter, ensuring safety and protection, offering emotional support, and advocating for the child's best interests.

In 1994, when I was 6 years old, my grandmother did all she could to care for us alone. When she contacted the state, we were all split up into different foster homes. No one was willing to take in a family of four ranging from 16 to 4 years old. We all went to the city of Carson, CA, which was only a 30-minute drive from my grandmother. Michelle went into one home, Amber into another, while they were able to keep Jaxon and me together. When children are put into the system, the first attempt is to find family members who are willing and able. Unfortunately for us, our grandmother was our only option.

Pulling up to the home of Rita and John Wright, I did not know what to expect. The neighborhood was clean, much different than what I was used to. It was a residential street where all the homes had manicured lawns, kids were outside riding bikes, and others played hopscotch on the sidewalk. Before entering the home, my first impression was, "Wow, this is going to be fun." Jaxon and I did not have toys of our own, but seeing other kids outside having a good time was enough for me. We had just come from Gma's senior citizen complex, which did not even allow children to live there, so we were always inside.

When we arrived at the Wright home, our assigned social worker walked us in to introduce us to our new foster parents. They greeted us at the front door with tight bear hugs, saying, "Welcome home," with the cheesiest smiles on their faces. The social worker reviewed a few things with us before leaving, assuring us we were in good hands. We were told there would be regular check-ins, visits with our grandmother and siblings, and phone time with our mother. As soon as the social worker pulled out of the driveway and the front door shut, our little lives turned upside down. All smiles disappeared. John did not say a word; he turned around and walked into their bedroom, as he often did. He was a man of few words. Rita, however, was the one in charge. She grabbed our bags and started giving us a tour of the house and a rundown of the rules.

From the front door to the left was the formal guest room, where the house phone was. She told us this was where we would take our phone calls with our social worker and mother. She told us she had another phone in the other room and would listen to all the calls. She warned us that if we ever mentioned how she ran her household, she would unplug the phone, and we would never talk to our mother again. The hallway led to their bedroom at one end and the two bedrooms we would be occupying in the other. Our first stop was the room assigned to me. She said, "This is where you will sleep. You will keep this room clean at all times." Pointing to a penguin piggy bank from the Batman collection, she added, "After all your chores are done, you will get an allowance but will not be allowed to spend it. You have to use this piggy bank to save your money." Next, we went into Jaxon's room, and she told him that the same rules applied and that he would be in trouble if he broke anything. She showed us the bathroom and all the other shared spaces in the home, reciting how she always expected the house to be pristine.

When we reached the kitchen, she showed us a walk-in pantry with a lock and key. It was filled with groceries, but she said we were not allowed to take anything unless she gave it to us or instructed us to get it. Then she took us to the backyard, explaining this was the only place we could be outside. We could not enter the front yard or play with the neighborhood kids. From the backyard, she led us into the garage, showing us, a large standing refrigerator filled with juices and sodas and a deep freezer with meat and tubs of ice cream. She told us nothing was there for us and that this should be the only time we entered. After the tour, she gave us a few more rules. She said she would enroll us in school the following week because she wanted to wait to see which school Amber would attend since she was in a nearby home. She did not want us to go to the same school. I did not understand why, but I just listened. She told me that I would be responsible for Jaxon, not her, and that I was expected to clean my room and the entire house every Saturday, including her bedroom.

It was a lot to take in, remember, and complete at six years old. I had never done chores before, and my older siblings had always watched over Jaxon and me. At that time, I only knew how to be a child, not a homemaker or caregiver. Things became very intense as the days turned into nights and the nights into days. I quickly realized that this was not what I thought it would be.

Once I started school, I was in the first grade and would come home with a weekly homework packet. Rita always made me sit at a small desk in the kitchen for hours, practicing my spelling words. She never helped me and said I should have asked the teacher before leaving school. I was learning how to read independently and was expected to understand instructions that included words I had never seen before. Education was important to Rita, but teaching was not one of her strengths. If I did not know the answer to a question or misspelled one of my spelling words during her home testing, she would lock me in the pantry for hours until I figured it out. I often went in there with the sunup and did not come out until bedtime, skipping dinner.

One time, one of my spelling words was "honey." I could not sound it out at all, so I went into the pantry. I remember crying silently because if she heard me, things would get physical. I sat there for hours, falling asleep and waking up, walking around in a small circle. Just by chance, I looked up and saw a box of Honey Nut Cheerios. I was so happy because I knew what that said, and my spelling word was "honey." I started banging on the pantry door to tell her I knew the word. When she opened the door, I said, "Honey, the word is honey." She asked if I had sounded it out, and feeling proud, I said I saw it on the cereal box. Before I knew it, her hand went across my face. She said, "I told you to sound it out," and locked the door again. That night was long; she left me in there until the next morning.

Rita had this unsettling ability to instantly transform her face from normal to demonic. Standing no more than 4'11" or 5'0" at most, she was pure evil.

I never understood how she could switch so easily. I returned from school one Friday afternoon but left my report card on my desk. Rita assumed I had deliberately left it behind because it was not good enough. Furious, she beat me mercilessly as though I were a grown woman off the streets. Her rage left me with two black eyes. It was the weekend, so I had some time to heal, but not completely. That Monday morning, she put makeup under my eyes to cover the faint bruising. She told me if anyone asked about my eyes to say that Jaxon and I were playing, and he accidentally kicked me in the nose. Unfortunately, no one asked, so nothing was said. When I got home that afternoon, I had my report card. During that time, the letter grades were O for outstanding, E for exceeding grade level, and S for satisfactory. My report card had Es for all subjects. This was one of the few times I saw Rita smile. That night, she took Jaxon and me to see Jurassic Park at the movie theater. It was our first theater experience.

Rita was not just strict about education; she also demanded a spotless house and expected instructions to be obeyed immediately. Any mistake was met with corporal punishment. One afternoon,

Jaxon and I played with action figures in the house. Rita kept an eye on Jaxon from another room and warned him not to break any toys. Sure enough, while playing too rough, Jaxon ripped off an arm of his action figure. He tried to hide it, but his body language gave him away. He was only four years old and did not know how to be sneaky.

Rita flew into a rage, snatched Jaxon off the floor by his shirt, and dragged him through the house to the backyard. Confused about what was happening, I followed her to the door and watched through the screen. She told Jaxon, "Since you like playing with broken toys, ride this bike." The bike was missing its seat, so she made him sit on the pole that held the seat and ride around the backyard until she told him to stop. He was crying and telling her it hurt his private parts, but she told him to shut up and keep riding. When Jaxon finally got off the bike, he could barely walk and had blood coming through his shorts. Later that night, he feared getting in at bath time because he was still hurting. I went into the bathroom to comfort him, and when Rita saw me, she said, "Since you're so strong, you go first." She let out the bath water already in the tub and turned on just the hot water. As the tub filled, steam rose from the water, and the mirror fogged up. I started to cry, knowing the water was too hot. I dipped my toe and pulled back when she told me to get in. She grabbed the back of my neck and forced me into the water. I screamed and hollered, splashing water everywhere as she attempted to submerge my entire body into the scalding water. This was only the first time; scalding baths became our regular punishment.

No matter what Jaxon and I did, it always resulted in some form of punishment. Most of the time, I took the worst of it because I was older and held responsible for Jaxon. Rita had a way of turning every situation into an issue. One day at school, I was surprised to see Amber there. I was so happy; I could not believe my eyes. We hugged each other tightly, jumping up and down and spinning all around. It had been months since I last saw her. I never knew why she switched schools; I did not care then. It was her third day there, and somehow, we had missed each other each day before. I had completely forgotten that Rita did not want us to be at the same school; she had only mentioned it once on our first night with her. Just before school ended that afternoon, Amber came by my hallway and gave me a doll. I could not wait to get home and play with it. The doll fell out of my bag when I got home and pulled out my homework. Rita asked me where I got it from, and I told her Amber had started going to my school and given it to me. At the time, Rita was standing near the refrigerator where the broom was kept between the fridge and the wall. Her face twisted into a demonic expression, and I instantly knew I had said something wrong. Without hesitation, she grabbed the thick wooden broom with straw bristles and swung it at my face. Knowing what was coming, I put my left arm up to block my face, and the broom hit my wrist, causing the bone to protrude through my skin. I still have that battle wound today. She never sought medical attention for any injury she inflicted; she would just use whatever home remedy she thought worked best. As she wrapped my arm, she told me if I ever told Amber anything, she would make sure I never saw her again. Of course, I listened—I was only a child.

Being so young, I could not distinguish Rita's threats from promises. Her favorite was to say, "If one of you answers any of the social worker's questions wrong, I will kill both of you." At that age, I believed everything, not realizing that if we had spoken a word about her wrongdoings, the social worker would have taken us away immediately. During the social workers' visits, we would all sit in the formal living room and catch up on how things had been from the last visit. Even John joined us, pretending to be involved in our daily lives. He went to work and then straight back to their bedroom. He never intervened or stopped Rita's madness. Part of the visit was just with Jaxon and me, allowing us to ask any questions or voice concerns. We never spoke up because we could feel the monster lurking on the other side of the wall. During one visit, the social worker commented on how much food was in the house, saying we must eat like football players with the amount of groceries for a household of four. If only I could tell her that most of it was the same food from her last visit. As Rita said, we were not allowed to have snacks or "her food." I remember Rita used to switch the food around before the social worker came, so it did not look the same.

Jaxon and I were not allowed to eat the same meals as Rita and John. Most nights, for as long as I can remember, our dinner consisted of plain black-eyed peas—just the beans and nothing more. The routine became so ingrained that I cannot recall it ever being different. I vividly remember the irony of preparing a meal for Rita and John, fully aware that I would be eating yet another bowl of warmed-up beans.

Sometimes, I would be in the kitchen, standing on a stool over the sink, peeling and deveining shrimp or peeling potatoes, silently hoping that tonight we might have some, too. Have you ever smelled something so perfectly seasoned that it seemed already cooked? That mouthwatering aroma alone would make my stomachache with longing. I could feel saliva rushing from the back of my jaws; the craving hit me so hard that it was almost painful. But the beans were always there, night after night, until the smell made my stomach turn. Eventually, I developed a gag reflex whenever I caught their scent. To this day, I would not say I like black-eyed peas.

On my birthday, I just knew dinner would be different. Nope, we had beans again, but this time, in celebration, we had a German chocolate cake for dessert. This was a treat, and both Jaxon and I fixated on that cake, knowing we had to finish our dinner first. Highly motivated, I started to eat the beans. About halfway through, I began to feel myself gagging. Before I knew it, I had thrown up right between my legs onto the floor. True to form, Rita had a dramatic outburst. While I was still in the chair, feet dangling, she pulled the chair back from the table, grabbed my bowl, and sat it on the floor, saying, "Put it in the bowl." I got on my knees, scraping the vomit off the floor back into the bowl. She then returned the bowl to the table and said, "Now finish your food." I cried because it was gross, but I knew there was no way out of it. After I finished, she lit the candles on the cake and sang "Happy Birthday" while I still had throw-up in my lap. Unfortunately, this is the first birthday I remember; I turned 7 years old.

Shortly after my birthday, Rita received an emergency placement for a baby boy who seemed to be around six months old. Initially, she was overjoyed to have the baby, but soon realized he was going through withdrawals and would not stop crying. She quickly grew tired of him and started leaving him in the room with me to care for. I had to feed, change, and bathe him like his mother. He became just another chore on my list. I had to grow up pretty fast living with Rita. She had me cook, clean, attend school, and care for two younger kids. The only time I had to be a child was in the playground at school.

During our stay with the Wright family, we had scheduled phone calls with my mother and grandmother and supervised visits. We never had any alone time on the phone or in person, so we could never disclose the abuse we were enduring. From the outside looking in, everything seemed fine, as if we lived in a happy, healthy, and loving environment. One day, Rita got a call from the agency asking if she could keep Amber for a few days because her foster parents had an out-of-state emergency. Rita was reluctant, but saying no would look suspicious. Before Amber arrived, Rita sat us down and explained that things would be different while Amber was visiting, I would not have to study as long, there would be no chores, and she would be cooking dinner. I did not realize it then, but now I know she was trying to portray a different environment for Amber because Amber was older and could report back on how we were being treated. Initially, things went well, but Amber's stay was extended, and Rita could not maintain the facade much longer. Little things started raising Amber's eyebrows. Amber stayed in the room with me and started asking questions one night. She could tell from my responses that I was hiding something. The next day, Rita was busy and told Amber to get something out of the freezer in the garage. When Amber got to the freezer, she saw all the tubs of ice cream and asked Rita if she could have some. Rita told her no.

Later that evening, Amber snuck into the garage and got some ice cream. When she returned, Rita noticed the ice cream on her shirt and asked about it. Amber admitted she had eaten it, and Rita immediately tried to attack her. But this time, she met her match. At 11 years old, Amber was the same height and nearly the same size as Rita, and she went toe to toe with her. John ran in and stopped them, but the night was chaotic. Amber was so enraged that she could not sleep, pacing back and forth, clenching her fists, and saying, "I can't wait to tell on her." She then looked at me and demanded the truth. I told her everything and felt safe for the first time in a long time.

The next morning, Rita had already removed the phone from the living room, so we could not call anyone. We stayed in the bedroom the entire day. The following day, it was time for Amber to go home, and Rita knew she was going to report the fight. Rita was nervous and scrambling, unsure of what to expect. Shortly after Amber went home, no more than an hour later, a social worker and my grandmother arrived at the front door to remove us from the Wright home. Because it was just the two of us, we were allowed to go home with Gma. Within a few days, we had a court hearing where Rita claimed that the only time, she ever laid a hand on me was when she caught me molesting the foster baby she had in her care. When I took the stand, and the judge asked me about Rita's accusation, it was clear that I did not know anything of that magnitude. I never knew what had happened in that situation, nor had I seen her face again after leaving the courtroom.

Chapter III

Home Sweet Home

One of my mother's greatest strengths is her determination. She has always got things done by any means necessary. If she did not accomplish something, it was because she chose not to. This became evident when we arrived at a four-bedroom house in Pasadena, California, just up the street from the famous Rose Parade route. It was our first home together after being in foster care. When my mother lost us to the state, she harnessed that determination to clean herself up, secure a job with the County, and obtain a fully furnished house to bring us back. We were not gone long because she did not linger in the streets or turn her back on us; she did what she had to do because she wanted us back.

The move-in day felt like a dream. The house seemed enormous; I was seven years old and about to start second grade. The house belonged to the church next door, and my grandmother's sister, a devoted member, persuaded the pastor to rent it to my mother. The property featured three yards: a front yard large enough for two houses, a yard between the house and the garage, and a spacious backyard with sugarcane plants and a kumquat tree. Walking in for the first time was like, wow. Straight ahead from the front door were the stairs, with a formal guest room and a study with an attached restroom to the right. To the left was the living room, which led into the kitchen. The kitchen was beautiful, featuring a three-way panel window overlooking the backyard, a large central island, and a nook off to the side. It also had what we called the side door, which was the most frequently used. The laundry room, also off the kitchen, had its own separate back door. All the bedrooms were upstairs initially until my mom made some renovations later. My mother had the main bedroom, Michelle's room was next to hers, and Amber and I shared the largest room, with Jaxon's room next to ours.

Everything we needed was already in the house. It was 1994, the year "The Lion King" had just come out. We had Lion King Sheets on the beds, character toothbrushes in the bathroom, and dressers with clothes already in the drawers. School had already started, so the neighborhood kids were not around when we arrived. However, we ran outside to meet them once school let out, and we heard the kids coming home. The first kids we met were our next-door neighbors, with whom we shared a fence. The oldest sister, Monica, was Amber's age; her brother Jacob was a year older than me, and they had a sister, Tonya, who was a year younger than me. There were not any kids Michelle's age around, and Jaxon stuck with me. I was a bit of a tomboy, so I became friends with Jacob and Tonya. There were two elementary schools about the same distance away in opposite directions. My mother enrolled us in the nicer one, so we did not attend the same school as our neighbors.

Our first year together and in the house went by quickly. The holidays passed, and more family started coming around. Life settled into a routine rapidly. My mother was working full-time, we were all in school, and we adapted to our new lifestyle, family, and friends. Every Saturday morning, Gma would come by bright and early to beat the traffic from LA to Pasadena. When it opened, she wanted to be the first person at the 99-cent store near our house. She would storm in, disregarding that it was Saturday morning, and we were allowed to sleep past 6 am. She would wake us up to get dressed, insisting there was no reason to sleep the day away. One ritual that was used with my grandmother was her ear checks. She would get a rag and clean our ears despite her long, pointy nails and rough approach if our ears were not clean. I liked going to the store with her because I knew I would get something, even though she warned me not to ask for anything. A dollar went a long way back then, especially in the 99-cent store, where candy bars were two for a dollar and small bags of chips were four for a dollar.

Sunday mornings were reserved for Sunday school and children's church. Since we shared a driveway with the church, we just walked over. I looked forward to grabbing my dollar and fifty cents from the kitchen counter on my way out. The dollar was for the offering, and the fifty cents was to buy a donut after Sunday school. I hate to admit it, but I most looked forward to the donut. We became heavily involved in the church, and getting baptized and joining the usher board was necessary. We also participated in vacation Bible school and choir.

For two years, Amber, Jaxon, and I attended Longfellow Elementary School before Amber graduated and moved on to middle school. Michelle was already at Pasadena High School. Those first two years were some of the bests. I was a pest of a little sister to Amber. My mother bought us matching outfits, and I always wanted to wear them on the same day. Amber would be so upset; I used to stall in the mornings before school just to see what she was wearing so I could put on the same thing. She hated it with a passion. She used to tell my mom it is embarrassing to dress like your little sister. I did not care; I thought she was cool at the time. She and all her friends would walk to school together, only allowing Jaxon and me to be ten feet ahead or behind. I guess they were talking about boys they liked or something. Longfellow is where I met friends who are still part of my life 30 years later. We are not on-the-phone types of friends, but social media keeps us in touch.

In third grade, when I was eight years old, my father returned to our lives. He had been struggling with drug addiction and had stayed away. I do not remember seeing him strung out, but Michelle and Amber, who knew him before I was born, talked about it. Reconnecting with my dad felt natural, as if no time had passed. Strangely, my only memory of him before his return was the only time he spanked me.

Both his mother, Grandma Louise, and my other grandma, Gma, lived in the same building. I was with my dad at Grandma Louise's house when Amber walked in with an orange from Gma's house. I asked her if she could walk me there to get one, but she said no. I was too young to go alone, so I went to Gma's house anyway. When I returned, my dad was sitting in a chair. He called me over, asking to see what I had. I showed him the orange, and he pulled a belt from behind his back, saying, "That's a tangerine," and struck me twice on the butt. I screamed, hollered, and wet myself. My father never hit me again, saying his voice was enough to make me nearly faint every time. He was a large man with a deep voice but never aggressive with me.

At this time, things changed. My dad, Mr. Samual Walkins, started picking me up more frequently, and life was great. Every Friday after school, he would pick me up for the weekend. He lived across the freeway in Inglewood. I still see myself running down the driveway, yelling, "Daddy!" as I jump into his arms. It happened the same way every week. I would skip the last two steps off the porch and take off. This was our routine during the school year, and I would stay with him for the summer. My dad, once a drug addict, had become a dealer. He started to have money, cars, and jewelry and enjoyed the finer things in life. I got my first debit card and pager when I was only nine years old. Christmases were good, and my birthdays became extravaganzas. We would ride the streets of Los Angeles like Bonnie and Clyde, though I did not know what was happening. My dad kept me close but out of the loop, always having something to entertain me while he conducted his shady business.

My dad was not your typical street guy; he was a gentle giant with a generous spirit. If he was doing well, everyone around him was too. He could not hear a sob story without trying to help. I remember waking up every morning to a hot breakfast. My dad made the best pancakes with crispy edges, the cheesiest eggs, and perfectly fried bacon. He was a great cook and a grill master. While he was known for his mac and cheese, my favorite meal was his roasted garlic baked chicken, mashed potatoes, spinach, and potato rolls. I can still taste the spinach, but I have never been able to duplicate it despite numerous attempts. We had favorite spots around town that will always hold special memories. Most Saturdays, we would go to Moby's Coffee Shop in Inglewood on Manchester, my favorite breakfast diner. Foster's Freeze had the best burgers and shakes, while Woody's BBQ had the best rib tips. And I cannot forget about Steven's in Gardena, which had the best pastrami in town.

My dad introduced me to fine dining, travel, money, and, most importantly, integrity. He always stood by his word. If he said he would do something, he did it. My dad taught me, without even trying, how to be a lady, how I should be treated, and the expectations I should set for a man by being himself and how he treated me. My dad loved me with all his heart. If you knew Samuel, you knew one thing for sure and two things for certain: he had a daughter named Kori, and I was his world. Whether I was around or not, I was always his main topic of conversation outside of business.

I remember before online banking; you had to go into a branch to deposit and transfer money. He opened my account when I was nine and gave me the card. Every time I needed money, he had to deposit it in the same branch because it was a Credit Union. Apparently, every time he went in, he would show everyone the latest picture of me. This bank was inside the Albertsons grocery store where he shopped, so naturally, he showed everyone around the store as well. I kid you not; I had only gone in there a few times over the years, but when I entered the store at around age 16, everyone from the butcher to the checkout clerks knew who I was by name and what I had been up to. My dad would update them as if they cared. The butcher even asked me how my competition went last week as if he had seen me recently. I loved that about my dad; he bragged about me, and I could do nothing wrong in his eyes.

Being with my dad was completely different from being with my mother. I was his only child at my dad's house, whereas I was one of four at my mom's house. Being the only child half the time, I developed some spoiled and brat-like tendencies. At my dad's, it was always about me, so I often got my way. I knew the difference and how to adjust my behavior with each parent. With my dad, we had special bonding moments and experiences. We had our little traditions, like walking to Baskin-Robbins instead of driving to get a pint of ice cream each to eat at midnight when MAD TV came on. We also enjoyed going to Blockbuster to rent movies, making stove-top popcorn over the fire, and melting butter in the microwave. In the summertime, he would even get into the pool and play Marco Polo with me. I learned how to swim the day he threw me into the 12-foot-deep end and said, "Sink or swim, either way, I got you." He was not actually in the pool but standing on the edge. I chose to swim.

My mother was quite different from my dad. She was no longer the outgoing person she used to be but preferred staying home in her room. Unlike my dad, she did not have fast money. Caring for four children full-time versus one part-time was a significant difference, and it showed. My mother's idea of taking us out was treating us to Sizzler's all-you-can-eat buffet maybe twice a year. It was not about money; it was more about convenience. There was no need to think about what to order or wait for the check. Whenever my mother took us anywhere, it always felt rushed and more like checking off a box than a genuine outing. Shopping trips were the same; she always seemed like she did not want to be there. Despite this, she still provided us with ways to entertain ourselves at home. We had a SEGA gaming system, and she turned the study into a game room with a pool table, a life-size dollhouse, racetracks, cars, and nearly every board game you could think of. She even saved all our Happy Meal toys and displayed them on shelves. It seemed like we got bikes every Christmas, which she would hide with sheets on Christmas Eve as if we could not see the wheels and handlebars. Now that I think about it, maybe she was just hiding the colors. We also had plenty of outdoor entertainment, with bikes, a basketball court in the backyard, and a garage equipped with a boombox for music.

Life was surprisingly good, and I felt normal. My mother began reconnecting with old friends she had known before her addiction, and extended family from my siblings' dad's sides started to come around. My mother's ex-husband, Brian's dad, somehow relates to Michelle's and Amber's dad. I am unsure of the connection, but the three share aunts and uncles with their fathers. My mother had a best friend named Mary, whom we called Aunt Mary. She was a foster mother with two biological children and, at the time, one adopted child. Her oldest son was grown and had left the house, but her oldest daughter, Shannon, was a year older than me, and her youngest daughter, Tyra, was a year younger. Aunt Mary often had a house full of foster girls. Shannon and I became best cousins. She would alternate between spending time with Amber and me depending on the circumstances. Amber, being older, had more freedom, whereas I was often unable to go anywhere because I was too young.

Chapter IV

467

Just when I thought life was good, it got even better. Aunt Mary moved from Lynwood to Pasadena, right around the corner from our elementary school. It was within walking distance, but we usually rode our bikes back and forth. This was fantastic because I saw my favorite cousins daily instead of just on weekends when they lived far away. Aunt Mary became the local connection my mother needed to show her there were more activities for us kids beyond just staying at home and in the neighborhood. She signed us up for the Boys and Girls Club, where we would go swimming, play games, do arts and crafts, and get away from the house.

We also had another aunt, Aunt Dee, who was a blood aunt to my three oldest siblings. We called her the road runner because she drove a large, school bus-sized van all over California. She loved driving and did not mind stopping by everyone's house to pick up the kids. She was the church-going aunt who only listened to gospel music, turned every song into a gospel version, and had us at every church event, from services to giveaways. She was so much fun to be around, but spending the night at her house was for the strong-hearted. Aunt Dee was not cut out for the kitchen respectfully. She could not cook to save her life. I remember we tried every tactic to avoid eating her food. There was no such thing as saying you were not hungry. She did not believe in going to bed hungry. If you asked to go to the restroom during a meal, she would check your mouth and hands for food to make sure you did not flush it. She would scoop it back together when you tried to spread the food around the plate to make it look like you had eaten. And forget about folding your plate or heading to the trash without her clearance. I never understood how she was the only adult who could not cook but always tried to feed us.

Growing up, our house was the central gathering place for holidays and celebrations. Every birthday,

Christmas, Thanksgiving, baby shower, or funeral repast, our house was where everyone gathered. The invitation was always extended to friends and even friends of friends. There was always enough for everyone. Depending on the season, either the men were outside on the grill, or my mother made pan after pan of delicious food in the kitchen. She preferred handling all the cooking herself, allowing guests to bring only desserts or drinks, but nothing that required the oven or stove. People were everywhere. The old folks were monitoring the food and to-go plates in the kitchen. The women were in the living room, gossiping about those not present and those within earshot.

The men were outside, drinking beer, reminiscing about their prime years and what they got away with. Kids ran around, throwing water balloons, and slipping and sliding in jelly sandals. The older kids would be upstairs in Michelle's room, which would be too cool for everybody in attendance downstairs. No matter what the occasion, there was always a performance by Amber, Shannon, and me. At one point, we thought we were TLC, but eventually, Amber aged out and was replaced by another cousin, and we became Destiny's Child. We would be in matching or color-coordinated outfits, performing original choreography that we had practiced for hours beforehand and solo acts. No one ever asked for a performance, but they always appreciated them.

Our house was not just one for gatherings; my mother had a soft spot for people who were displaced or transitioning. Knowing what I know now, I can understand why. Jaxon's father was a carpenter who worked on all types of construction throughout Los Angeles. He worked on the house, and my mother made the once study and turned the game room into a bedroom. Instead of separating Amber and me, she had a guest room that always had a guest. She would house family members, friends, or family members of friends, and sometimes Michelle and Amber's friends when they were put out, and whoever else she met needed a roof. I heard whispers when I was younger that there were always ulterior motives behind her helping hand, but I was one to stay out of grown folks' business.

My mother had a friend named Vickie, whom she met through work; they were in the same training class. They became close, though I still do not quite understand their dynamic, as they are two completely different women. Vickie is mild-mannered, soft-spoken, and private, whereas my mother is very opinionated, judgmental, and sometimes vulgar. Vickie takes a special liking to Jaxon and eventually becomes his godmother. She would come over during the week to help Jaxon with his homework, and on weekends, she would pick him up and spend the day driving around, visiting various stores, and going from one drive-thru to the next.

During that time, Vickie faced some financial struggles, which I believe were due to her self-discipline and efforts to better position herself. She minimized her living arrangements and let go of non-essentials like cable TV. I completely misunderstood her situation because I was young and unaware of real-life responsibilities. Vickie would come over on a specific day of the week at the same time to watch her favorite show, "Bewitched." I could not stand it. We always had to give up the TV, be quiet, or leave the living room so she could watch her show. I used to get so upset and ask why she could not watch TV at home.

I became so annoyed that I would do little mean things when I saw her coming. I used to unscrew the cable plug just enough, so it did not work, but it still looked connected. No one knew how to fix it but me. If my mother were not home when she arrived, I would sometimes turn everything off, lock the doors, and pretend no one was home until she left. Most times, she would wait in her van until my mom arrived. Looking back, I cannot believe I did those things because, over the years, Vickie has become more of a mother to me than I ever had.

With all the comings and goings, my mother kept a spotless house. Stepping inside, you would never guess four children lived there. We had rotating chores: during the week, we focused on the kitchen, while weekends were dedicated to everything from scrubbing walls and baseboards to wiping the railing and sweeping the stairs. My mother did not allow us to use her washing machine, so she did all the laundry herself. She would wash and fold the clothes, stack them neatly on the kitchen island, and call us to pick them up. Sometimes, her laundry routine was a bit stressful. If I wore something on Monday and found it back in my drawer by Friday, I could not remember if I had worn it that week or the week before. If we had company during the week, everyone knew to start tidying up 15 minutes before my mother got home from work. When she arrived, we would sit quietly until she had walked through the door, gone straight to her bedroom, and changed into her well-known housedress. We could move about again after she decompressed and shook off the day. If things were not in order, the consequence was that our company had to leave. There were days when the day had been too overwhelming, and she did not want to deal with us, let alone anyone else's children.

For the most part, having company around kept sibling rivalry to a minimum. At first, when we were all reunited, the atmosphere felt warm and loving. I remember Michelle loved combing my hair, and Amber would sing "Silent Night" at bedtime until I fell asleep. At that time, they were my big sisters, to whom I looked up. As time went on, things changed, and so did our dynamics. I understood that as they got older, their interests changed, and friends became more important. Michelle had her own room, so I was not allowed in when her friends were over unless she invited me to show off some new dance moves. Then, back out the door, I went.

Amber, who is only four years older than me, always acted much older. She did not like to come out and play; she preferred to stay cute and well-dressed at all times. To this day, she is the only person I know who combs her hair and puts on lip gloss before bed.

As I continued spending weekends and summers with my dad, my relationship with my sisters grew more distant. I did not mind then because my cousin Shannon moved to Pasadena with her mom while her dad stayed in Inglewood. Shannon and Tyra had the same weekend schedule as me. Our dads were friends and occasional business partners who lived just around the corner from each other. Shannon and I were inseparable, even when we were not at home. I was either at her dad's place, or she was at mine. We spent our days together, whether being dropped off at the mall, the movies, the beach, or Knott's Berry Farm—you name it, we were there.

We loved being at our fathers' houses because we had no structure. They were amazing men who spoiled us endlessly. We did not have chores or responsibilities with them; they cared for everything for us.

Coming home on Sunday nights after spending the weekend with my dad, I was never empty-handed. I always returned with something new: clothes, shoes, toys, or a story. Looking back, I can imagine how that might have made my siblings feel, but at the time, I was just a happy kid eager to show off my new things or talk about my adventures. My dad never excluded my siblings when they were around; he was always fair and would help my mother out when needed. He did not do as much for them as he did for me because I was his only responsibility. My Christmas and birthdays looked slightly different because my mother had to shop for all of us, whereas my dad only had to shop for me. Some years, I spent the holidays traveling to visit my dad's family in Oklahoma and spent summers in Texas. Looking back, this may have driven a wedge between my sisters and me. Out of nowhere, they became more irritated with me and would say and do things to get me in trouble. It was far from where we started, especially with Amber more than Michelle.

Amber would do sneaky things, like drinking my mother's last Pepsi and blaming me for it, fully aware it would cause a huge fuss. Every year for Valentine's Day, Jaxon's dad would bring my mother a box of chocolates, and every year she bought us small heart-shaped boxes of chocolates. One year, she ran behind and had to go to the store to get our candy. While she was gone, Amber entered her room (violation number one), opened my mother's chocolates, and ate a piece (violation number two). When my mother returned, she called us all down and asked who had done it. Naturally, we all looked confused and proclaimed our innocence. She made us go back to our rooms until someone confessed.

Amber told me she had done it but suggested I would not get in as much trouble if I confessed. Amber was a bit chubby, and my mom hated that, so I understood why she might get in more trouble for sneaking a piece of candy. Amber promised that if I got punished, she would stay inside with me. As soon as I looked my mother in the face and started to speak, she struck me across the face and said, "You go to your room, and the rest of you can go back outside." Amber took off running out the door, leaving me to take the blame for her wrongdoing.

I got a lot of whippings for falling for Amber's nonsense. It seemed like my mother was more upset with me for being gullible than with Amber for being mischievous and mean. Amber once dared me to climb out the upstairs bedroom window and sit on the ledge beneath it. As soon as I climbed out the window and before I could even sit down, I heard the window slam shut, the lock click, and the blinds drop. I was crying and banging on the window, convinced Amber was on the other side. Moments later, I saw her running down the driveway, laughing and waving goodbye. By some miracle, my mother came upstairs to put something in the linen closet and heard me outside. Of all people, she was the last person I wanted to find me. I immediately started tattling on Amber, but my mother stayed silent. She grabbed her belt and started disciplining me.

When I was younger, my biggest fear was the movie "Candyman." If you said his name three times in the mirror, he would appear and kill you. If I had to use the restroom at night, I would never flush the toilet because of the noise. Whenever I took a bath, I would leave the bathroom door cracked. The bathroom had one of those oval medicine cabinets that protruded from the wall, so you could see the hallway if the door were open. The light switch was outside the bathroom. One time, Michelle and Amber pulled the door shut, held it tight, turned off the lights, and whispered "Candyman" through the door. I completely panicked, desperately trying to get out of that bathroom. Water was everywhere because I had just rushed out of the bathroom. Unbelievably, I got a whipping for my reaction.

Michelle and Amber were older; they didn't get whippings like Jaxon and me. I could endlessly share stories and situations where I ended up with the short end of the stick for no reason. Eventually, I started to catch on to their tricks and stopped falling for the okie doke. Once Michelle and Amber realized I had caught on, they began saying things to hurt my feelings or get under my skin. Their go-to comeback whenever they were upset with me was, "That's why Samuel isn't your real dad." They used to say it so often and with such conviction. Every time, I would run to my mother crying, and she never corrected them or disciplined them. She always said, "They're only saying that because they're mad." I believed my mother because I had never known anything different.

Chapter V

Writing on the Walls

Home life started to get a little rocky as time went on. My mother was not involved in whatever we had going on. Her routine consisted of going to work, coming home, and watching "Law & Order" while smoking cigarettes and drinking Pepsi. If I had to guess, cooking was probably the only thing she enjoyed outside of that and gossiping. She was a great cook, which brought her a lot of recognition.

Another thing my mother was known for was prioritizing appearances. She did not attend back-to-school nights, review our homework, or schedule regular doctor's appointments. We hardly ever went to the doctor, even when we were sick.

There was a time when Amber had a severe strep throat infection, and when my mother finally took her to the doctor, he said she was hours away from meeting her Maker. Another time, I was outside rollerblading when my mom told me to come inside. Being a kid, I did one more circle around the rose bush and fell while trying to brace my fall with my hands. When I came into the house crying, my mother remained unfazed. I cried for hours, telling her I could not move my arm or hand and that the pain was unbearable, but she did not react. Later, Brian called from prison and heard me crying in the background. Somehow, he convinced my mother to take me to the emergency room. Of course, my wrist was broken. My mom was furious that we had to wait so long and even more upset that there would be a follow-up visit.

Family members noticed my mother's lack of interest in us and started to pick us up, take us on errands, and sometimes have us spend the night. It really took a village. It was not that my mother was not capable; she just had no desire to be involved. She was set in her way and did not hesitate to say whatever was on her mind or do what she felt. She believed she was right if she thought of it, came up with it, or did it. In her mind, no one could match her logic level because she was so smart and witty.

Whenever my mother did or said something outrageous, I knew she had thought it through and did not care.

Every holiday, my mother would tell the same story about having me. She always found a way to bring it up, not wanting to miss the chance to share it. In short, she learned of her pregnancy with me quite late. She had an irregular menstrual cycle and was petite, so she just was not aware. When she found out, she searched high and low for a doctor who would perform a risky two-day procedure. When she finally found a doctor who wanted to do the abortion, that same day, she felt me move. At that point, the abortion was out, and she had to have me. And I quote, "When I saw this little ugly redhead baby, I knew nobody would love her, so I kept her," before continuing that she was ready to put me up for adoption. Depending on who was at the table, some people would laugh, while others would look awkward.

Initially, my mother's holiday story did not bother me because when she first started telling it, I was young and did not fully grasp what she was saying. I thought it was one of those "look at God" moments. It was not until I got a little older that I began to understand and feel uncomfortable hearing it. I remember the first time I asked my mother why she treated me differently from my siblings. I was about eight years old. I cannot recall what made me ask, but I clearly remember her response: "You have your dad, so you don't need me like the others do." At that age, I just accepted it. Around the age of ten or eleven, I started to pay more attention to certain things, including her story, and began to feel unwanted. I cannot recall specific actions, but the feeling was strong. It was not just at home that I felt this way; my Grandma Louise gave me the same eerie feeling.

My dad was Grandma Louise's only child; they were genuinely best friends. Wherever one was, the other was always nearby. They either lived together, in the same apartment complex, or on the same street. They never strayed far from each other. Being with my dad meant I was often with Grandma Louise, too. She did not go out and about with us, but she was always home when we returned with something fresh off the stove and a homemade dessert from the oven. Dinner always comes with dessert.

Grandma Louise married Grandpa Dave; I never knew my dad's biological father. Grandpa Dave could sometimes be intimidating, but we also had our bonding moments. He was a World War II veteran, honorably discharged with a Purple Heart. He spent his days watching old black-and-white western movies and rarely left the house, alternating between the bedroom and the living room. He had this desk chair in the living room that was big enough for me to curl up in and spin around. He always told us not to play in his chair, and whenever he caught us doing so, he would throw a pocketknife into the wall to get our attention without saying a word. We definitely got the message. Other times, he would let me play with his long, straight hair when I was learning to braid, and I would walk alongside him in his electric wheelchair to get his favorite black walnut ice cream. The intimidating part was that he was a man of few words, but you always knew when he was angry or just being his normal self. I cannot say I have ever seen him show happiness or excitement.

I never really had bonding moments with Grandma Louise. She had a goddaughter, My'Kisha, who was the same age as me and whom she clearly favored.

My'Kisha lived closer to Grandma Louise, so she was around her more often. Every time I visited, My'Kisha would be there. We got along well and practically grew up together, but even then, I could tell things were different between My'Kisha and me. Grandma Louise barely spoke to me when I was alone at my grandmother's house without My'Kisha. She made sure I was fed and had my shower, but beyond that, I just waited for my dad to come home.

When My'Kisha was around, I was even more invisible. We could both play on the living room floor, and Grandma Louise would ask My'Kisha if she wanted to go to the store with her. If I asked to go along, she would give me a look that clearly said no, even though she never said it outright. After swimming, she would wash and comb My 'Kisha's hair but leave mine matted. If she bought something for My'Kisha and not for me, she would always say it was up to My'Kisha whether she wanted to share. On Sundays, when we went to church, My'Kisha always got to sit in the front seat, even if I called it first. They played cards and dominoes together and watched their favorite shows, and Grandma Louise even let her help in the kitchen. As for me, I was just my daddy's child.

A lot of her favoritism went over my head because my dad did an amazing job of ensuring I was always happy. He would take me to the salon when my hair was not washed. He would redirect my attention to something else if he noticed any difference in how she treated me. It was not until I got older that I realized what she was doing and how he tried to smooth things over without bluntly defending me. Over the years, I only heard my dad and Grandma Louise argue about me once. My dad came into a lump sum of money and gave her a portion, but he gave me a larger portion to put into my savings account. She was livid, upset that he had given me so much and not her. She said things like, "Now you're taking this too far," and something about putting me above his mother. I did not hear much, but I got the gist of it. All I knew was after that argument, things got worse, and she started to act like my being around was an issue. When she would talk to other people, it seemed like she made it a point to compare My'Kisha and me.

The excitement to see my dad was always high, but it began to dwindle once I arrived at his house for the weekend. I stopped looking forward to going because I knew my grandmother would find a way to be upset with me, so she did not have to deal with me. If she weren't in a mood, we would go to her sister's house, my great aunt's, for small gatherings. She would always boast about My'Kisha, saying things like, "You know My'Kisha is learning Spanish in school, while this one is just wasting time gyrating." I was a cheerleader then, but to Grandma Louise, there was no future in that. It was just a gateway to other unruly behaviors.

I had two male cousins, one a couple of years older and one the same age as me. They lived full-time with my great-aunt, who was their grandmother. We used to play together all the time, and sometimes, my dad would take them swimming with us to get them out of the house. Grandma Louise always insisted that I needed to be watched around them because I was "hot in the tail." I found this gross—they were my cousins, and besides, I was more of a tomboy than they were when I was not in my cheerleading outfit.

My'Kisha was the one into boys; she even had a crush on my older cousin since she was not technically family. Grandma Louise was so busy watching me that she did not notice how advanced My'Kisha was. I remember one day, My'Kisha and I were playing outside at Grandma Louise's house with the neighborhood kids, most of whom were boys. I was the youngest by a year or two, but these kids were much more advanced than me. They wanted to play a game called hide and go get it. Once I learned that if you were caught, you had to do something freaky, I was out—I was not interested.

My'Kisha played and got caught in the laundry room by maybe three or four boys. I could not quite make out what was happening when I peeked in because I got scared and looked away. Soon after, a neighbor knocked on my grandmother's door, saying she caught My'Kisha in the laundry room with several boys with their pants down. I cannot say what actually happened, but I know she got the whooping of a lifetime. I felt sad for My'Kisha but also a bit relieved that Grandma Louise's perfect godchild was not so perfect. Although Grandma

Louise loved to stay on the phone, this incident stayed in-house.

Chapter VI

Pre-teen

Finally! My elementary days are over. I attended Longfellow Elementary School through the sixth grade. While that might sound typical, the middle school I was zoned for also included sixth graders. If my mother had let me go there, I could have gone to school with my cousin Shannon and all her foster sisters. Instead, I was still with the little kids, wearing barrettes and beads.

In seventh grade, I attended Elliot Middle School in Altadena, CA. I was excited to be out of elementary school and among the older kids. Shannon and I were reunited, and now that we were back at the same school, I could spend nights at her house during the week and take the bus to school in the morning. We used to have so much fun at the bus stop, changing the lyrics to Usher's song, singing, "It's seven o'clock on the dot, we're at the bus stop." We were thick as thieves. Since Shannon had been at Elliot a year ahead of me, she had developed new friendships and started hanging out with them more frequently. Eventually, I met other kids from neighboring elementary schools who started at the same time as I did, and I also began to form new friendships. Shannon and I grew apart at school but remained very close at home.

Middle school is where most pre-teens start to find themselves. For me, I was just as lost as the day I started. I do not believe I found myself at Elliot. Where I lived, I was in the middle of two school zones. Elliot was not prestigious by any means, but it was not really ghetto like the opposing school, Washington Middle School. At Elliot, most of the kids came from Altadena, a Pasadena suburb. Altadena is known to have higher-income homes and a more financially stable community. The kids attending Elliot were somewhat spoiled in comparison; they had all the latest fashions and gadgets. At Washington, the community was more deprived and near the housing projects. Most kids at Washington who had the latest and the greatest came from families hustling in the streets.

Before going to Elliot, I thought we lived a decent life. I was okay with shopping at Sears and Burlington for school clothes and Payless for shoes. My thought process at the time was quantity over quality. I was never into Jordans and Nikes because I would only get one or two pairs versus four pairs at Payless if I chose those. In middle school, things changed. Kids were now paying attention to what you wore and making fun of what you did not have. I remember everybody was wearing GAP sweaters at one point, and I wanted one so badly. This was the first time I realized shopping at those stores was not optional; it was what my mother could afford between us.

Being in middle school exposed me to much more than I was ready for. I always thought I was in the know or on track with my peers, but apparently, not only was I behind in fashion, but I was also behind on the social meter. Without even knowing it, I was sheltered. My mother was older than my classmates' parents. For that, I could not have the same freedom as others. Meeting new friends and learning their way of hanging out and having a good time was vastly different from what I was used to. Going into middle school, I was still a tomboy who happened to love dancing. I was friends with the guys because of our shared interest in sports, but I was also friends with many girls because of dance. Before middle school, I had never encountered anything beyond an elementary school crush. He used to chase me down and hit me because he liked me.

At Elliot, those of us without extracurricular activities would usually walk up the street to Jack in the Box after school to hang out. After practice, we would all head over to the library. Back then, the Altadena Library was where many people had their first kiss or other memorable first experiences. It was not apparent to me right away that kids my age were already sexually active. I remember meeting this one girl; we hit it off in one of our classes. After a few weeks, we started walking home together and building a closer bond. This girl was way beyond my level of comprehension. The first time I heard Ludacris, "What's your fantasy?" she was rapping it word for word. It blew my mind. I knew then she was different, with no judgement passed. Later during the year, she started ditching school to see an older guy she met on the party line. This scared me for so many reasons; obviously, it was dangerous, but she was also going across the freeway to LA while she was supposed to be in school. At this time, the most I had ever done was pretend to be sick when a new Michael or Janet Jackson video came out so I could stay home and learn the dance moves.

After mixing and mingling throughout the school year, I made more friends and, ironically, a few enemies. I do not remember any specifics, but I recall a few girls who annoyed me just by their mere existence. I am sure they must have rubbed me the wrong way at some point. There was one girl with whom I shared my gym class. I am unsure what her issue was with me, but she always had something disparaging to say—not directly to me, but loud enough for me to hear and know it was about me. One afternoon in gym class, tensions boiled over. Once we entered the locker room to change, she did something she must regret to this day. When we started fighting, I believe she may have touched every locker in that room, and someone had to peel her off the floor when I was done with her. I literally turned her every which way but loose. This was not my first fight, but it was my first showcase. My first fight was over double-dutch with my next-door neighbor's cousin. I picked a fight with her, and she wore me out all through the gravel on the ground. That was when my mother told me, "The day you start a fight is the day you will lose a fight." I took that to heart and never started another fight, but every fight after that was a victory.

After my locker room incident, people became noticeably friendlier, eager to ensure we were on good terms rather than adversaries, except for one girl, Maya Duncan. Maya and I shared the same gym class, and while she had been front and center during my altercation, she never uttered a word. In fact, we had never spoken to each other at all, but there was always this unspoken look of mutual acknowledgment when we passed each other in the halls.

Like most schools, Elliot had a basketball team anyone could join, though purchasing the uniform was required. At the time, basketball was everything to me. I would play from sunrise to sunset on the weekends and spend hours after school perfecting my game. I was so obsessed with Shaquille O'Neal when he played for Orlando that, in the fourth grade, I secretly wore my Shaq jersey for picture day without an undershirt. My mother was furious when she saw the pictures, but I was beaming with pride. I tried out for the school team, made it, and practiced for weeks. But when it was time to pay for the uniform, my dad was nowhere to be found, and my mother did not have the money. She told me that school should be free and that I was out of luck if it was not.

I was hurt, but more than that, I was embarrassed that I had to quit the team because we could not afford the uniform. A day or two later, I overheard my mother on the phone, agreeing to loan someone more money than the uniform cost. I knew better than to question her, so I just went to the backyard and dribbled my basketball around with tears streaming down my face, trying to convince myself that she truly did not have it when I asked. I could not think of any other reason she would say no.

As it turned out, my backyard practice sessions paid off. My great-uncle, who lived next door, had a close friend who frequently visited, and that friend happened to be the head basketball coach at Washington Middle School. He scouted me, telling my uncle he could use me on the school's basketball team. Although I attended Elliot, he managed to arrange for me to play for Washington after school. It was an easy decision, and he secured my spot on the team. The school was within walking distance from my house, and he even offered to pay for my uniform.

The following week, I started leaving my school immediately after the last bell, catching the first bus to make it to practice on time. The coach did not cut me any slack just because I had to travel; practice began exactly one hour after the last bell. If I was late, no matter the reason, suicide drills were guaranteed. On days when my mother did not give me bus fare, I had to hustle to the free bus stop, which only got me partway, and then sprint the rest of the way on foot. Whether I was running to get to practice on time or running during practice as punishment for being late, I was always on the move.

I only played at Washington for one season. I did not get the support I had hoped for—neither my mother nor father ever attended my games or were willing to take me to travel games. It felt awkward constantly asking teammates for rides and never having anyone in the stands cheering me on. Even after the season ended, I continued going to Washington after school because my next-door neighbors were part of the dance team. Since dance was right up my alley, I joined the after-school program with them. Hanging out at Washington was where I got my first glimpse of the rougher side of Pasadena. These kids were a whole different crowd. Even though I lived just minutes away from the Housing Projects, Jackie Robinson Park, and La Pintoresca, I never spent time there. But before I knew it, hanging out with the Washington crew had me right in the thick of it.

Middle school was where I realized I was a chameleon, adaptable, and able to blend into any environment. I began to see that I did not fit into just one box. I had friends from all walks of life, from the nerdiest kids to the coolest jocks and everything in between. I could relate to everyone on some level. I was the kind of kid who was interested in everything and good at many things. If something were not working, I could fix it; if it were broken, I could repair it; and if it were complicated, I was determined to figure it out.

Balancing the different lifestyles between school and home came naturally to me. The home served as the bridge between the two. At Elliot, I had the structure to excel academically and maintain proper behavior. However, I gained the street smarts at Washington to hold my own. One day, after dance practice at Washington, I fought with another student. I cannot remember what sparked it, but she approached me first. Feeling justified, I stood my ground and fought back. She had what we used to call French braids, now known as scalp braids. I grabbed her braids during the fight and landed uppercuts as she knelt. Eventually, she managed to pull away, ripping her hair from the scalp. She ran off crying, threatening to bring her family.

Not long before I could leave the block, her mother and other family members arrived. Her mother forced us to fight again, and as I got the upper hand, she jumped in, and I ended up fighting both. It was my first time confronting an adult physically; I was only in the seventh grade and had never even argued with an adult before. Both the mother and daughter walked away battered and bruised.

The next day at my school, I was called into the Dean's office. The phone was on speaker, and the Dean from Washington was on the line. Word about the fight had spread, and it had reached the staff at Washington, who then contacted my school to inform them that I was no longer welcome to participate in any of their afterschool programs. My school took it a step further, called my mother to let her know what had happened, and informed her that I was suspended for three days.

After the incident at Washington, I began spending more time with the kids I went to school with. Remember that girl, Maya Duncan, from my gym class? Strangely enough, she and I ended up becoming friends.

Chapter VII

Maya Duncan

Back when I was in middle school, we had seven classes instead of the four students have now. The gym has always been my favorite, although we call it PE, which is short for physical education. My gym teacher was a young, energetic Black woman, probably in her late twenties at the time. She was one of the cooler, more relatable teachers. I vividly remember when she organized a group of girls, including myself, to dance at the school talent show. We danced to Erykah Badu's hit song "Bag Lady." At the time, I did not understand why she chose such a slow song, but looking back now with the wisdom of experience, I realize she might have been going through something that flew right over our heads.

Even though my gym teacher was great, and the gym was my favorite class, I did not participate as I should have. Instead of actually changing into my gym clothes, I'd just put them on over my regular clothes to get credit for dressing out. When it came time for physical strength tests, like pull-ups and push-ups, I always had an excuse to sit out. On mile run days, I spent most of the time walking the track with two other girls, making up songs. We were convinced we would be the next big girl group. I did not have the best singing voice, but I could hold a note and choreograph a pretty solid dance routine.

As we strolled around the track, Maya Duncan would suddenly sprint past us like a lightning bolt. She could easily run a mile in under five minutes and never seemed tired, as if she were born to be a track star. Maya was always quiet, with a resting expression that said, "Don't talk to me," without her ever saying a word. Maya was not friendly or inviting in the slightest. One day in gym class, I tried talking to Maya, and she seemed irritated by my presence. Strangely enough, I felt an immediate connection. She did not feel the same at first, but for some reason, I liked her. She never tried to fit in, stayed out of drama, and, unlike most people, did not treat me any differently after my locker room fight. She was flat-out mean, and I respected it. I had never met another kid of my age who was so straightforward; she was interesting. There was something mysterious about her; her expression always seemed to say something that made me curious about what was going on in her mind. Initially, I would talk to her just because I knew it annoyed her, but over time, it turned into one of those situations where she had no choice but to warm up to me. My small talk gradually evolved into full-blown conversations.

We were full-fledged friends by the time we reached eighth grade; she was the yin to my yang. We were completely opposites but somehow the same. We were both Leos, and her birthday was just one day before mine, which made us feel like twins. Her thoughts were mine, and mine were hers. We could have entire conversations just with our eyes, fully understanding each other without saying a word. Everything was always hilarious to us. We would talk on the phone for hours; we were hanging out together when we were not talking. Our friendship felt destined, like she was a handpicked sister. We knew we were opposites but always accepted each other for being exactly who we were.

2001 Maya and I finally reached ninth grade at Pasadena High School. It felt like we had been waiting for this moment forever. Neither of us had been too interested in boys in middle school. We had an occasional crash, but nothing serious. But high school was a whole different story. Our eyes were suddenly wide open. We could not believe the sight of our school's basketball team. Those boys were fine, especially the varsity players. You see, something we had never seen up close before is what they had in place; they practically already had their grown man build. We quickly started daydreaming and picking out our favorites, even though they were juniors and seniors who barely noticed us. To keep things discreet, we would refer to them by code names whenever we talked about them, which was all the time.

Eventually, our code names expanded beyond just the basketball team and became how we referred to everyone. Since Maya and I did not share many classes, we used a composition book to write notes back and forth. We would exchange it during every passing period, discussing everything under the sun. That book was like our secret world, and we guarded it carefully. Even if it ever fell into the wrong hands, we felt safe because there were no real names; only we could decipher it, except for that one time when a teacher confiscated it and read it aloud in class. Maya had written about a classmate, using a code name, saying he did not bathe because he still had the same writing on his hand from the day before. The class had no idea who she meant, but I knew, and so did that classmate. That was the closest we ever came to being exposed. We talked about many people in that book, and I thank God, we kept it close.

Maya and I carried the same personality from middle to high school. She remained sharp and guarded while I was still the social butterfly. Some of the kids I started hanging out with from Washington Middle School also transitioned to Pasadena High, including many people Maya did not know. In true Maya fashion, she was not interested in getting to know them. I bounced between separate groups. So, naturally, Maya would spend time with others with whom she was familiar. The only real tension came between Maya and my male best friend, Tylan Reed. They just could not get along for some reason, but I loved and valued them equally.

As much fun as Maya and I had during our first year, going to basketball games, attending pep rallies, and proudly chanting '05, everything shifted by the second semester; my life at home changed drastically, and it began to take a toll on me mentally and emotionally. For as long as I can remember, my mother always left our lunch money and bus fare on the kitchen island for us to grab before heading to school. But over time, that money started to shrink and eventually stopped altogether. I began showing up at school without any money, unable to buy lunch or snacks like I used to, and sometimes I had to walk home or ask for a free ride when I did not have bus fare. Things continued to get worse. I no longer kept up with the latest fashion and started wearing the same shoes repeatedly, so they began to smell from getting wet in the rain. My father would go missing from time to time, which meant he was in jail. He never had any hard time, nothing more than 30 days. I always felt his absence, though. Other times, he would be so heavy in the streets that weeks would go by without a visit.

I never told Maya about the changes at home because I was too ashamed to discuss them. However, it was clear to her without needing any explanation. Maya must have noticed the changes at my house when she visited and began looking out for me without making things awkward. At school, she started sharing her snacks or pretending she did not want them so she could give them to me. After school, she began offering me rides home when she saw I was not taking the bus. Her mother was incredibly kind, always willing to give me a ride and eventually even pick up food before dropping me off. They never made me feel different, so I did not realize what they were doing until much later when I understood that Maya had known my secret all along. She never asked, hinted, eluded, or pried into the obvious changes in my life; she and her mother just silently shifted into looking out and making sure I was good whenever I was around.

As my home life began to take a toll, I started lashing out at anyone who looked at me the wrong way or said something I did not like. Although Maya was the one to say things like, "Why are you talking to me?" or "Don't talk to me; I don't like you," I constantly got into altercations, often fighting nearly every day. Ironically, the locker room fight was the only one Maya witnessed. Every time I fought, she seemed to have just left or arrived at the end. In addition to fighting, I became rebellious, skipping class, coming, and going as I pleased, and doing whatever I wanted. I became disobedient and disrespectful, running my own show. Eventually, the school had enough and sent me to continuation school.

Now that Maya and I were no longer attending the same school, our relationship was not strayed; we still talked on the phone and hung out occasionally, but not nearly as much as we did. We both began to grow closer to other people, but without a shadow of a doubt, we were still best friends and sisters for life.

Chapter VIII

The Spiral

From the moment my siblings and I were reunited with our mother after foster care, I carried an unspoken fear of being taken from her. From the age of seven until I was fourteen, I often fell asleep in my own bed, only to wake up in my mother's bed the next morning. It was not just me; Amber and Jaxon did the same thing. We would all end up piled together in her king-size bed. I am not sure why they did it, but for me, it was not about being afraid of my own bed or the dark; it was the fear of being unable to be with her. I feared the memories of foster care and the nights that I cried for her, and she was not there.

My time with the Wrights instilled a fear in me that would affect any child. Being smart, helpful, and productive helped me survive in their home. As long as I kept up with that, I could avoid some form of punishment or physical abuse. When I returned to my mother, I carried those same lessons with me and tried to apply them to her.

However, my mother was not easily impressed by the actions she believed were expected of me. With the kind of relationship we had, I desperately wanted to be her shining star. At this age, I recognized my mother had difficulties loving me the same way as my siblings, but I craved her love so much that I did the opposite of what Michelle and Amber did to disappoint her. When both of them dropped out of high school, I knew I had to be the one to finish and give her that graduation ceremony.

During the first semester of ninth grade, things started to feel unstable. Home life shifted from what we had known for the past seven years. My mom grew more irritable than usual, and her interest in parenting seemed to vanish. She went from waking us up for school to asking if we planned to go. Home-cooked meals were replaced with frequent pots of Hamburger Helper, and lunch money became a thing of the past. Anything beyond basic necessities was an absolute no.

There were not any obvious signs of why things had changed; it happened so gradually that it went practically unnoticed. At the time, it just seemed like one of those rough patches' adults go through while trying to make ends meet. My mother never talked about bills, finances, or hardships. We just had what we had, and that was that. No questions were asked, and no explanations were given.

One night, a phone call that lasted less than 30 seconds changed the course of my life from that point on. Back then, all we had were house phones, and if you had a call waiting, you could place one call on hold to answer another. However, the phone would ring loudly if you hung up the second call without clicking back over.

That night, I was on the phone past my allowed time. My mother's uncle, who lived next door, called to speak with her. It was unusual for him to call since he would normally just walk over. I had to listen to their conversation so that when my mother hung up, I could quickly switch back on my call and avoid the phone ringing, keeping me from being caught on the line after hours.

While eavesdropping on the phone call, I heard my mother's uncle say, "I put it in the mailbox." I was baffled hearing this and was like, what could he possibly leave in the mailbox that he couldn't just bring into the house? Our mailbox was at the bottom of the front porch steps; ten more steps, and he could have easily delivered it to the door. My mother had just gotten out of the shower and said, "Let me put something on, and I'll go get it."

Before she could, I rushed down the stairs and out the kitchen door, heading straight for the mailbox. When I opened it, my heart shattered. My chest pounded, my hands trembled, and a knot tightened in my throat. Hearing the front door unlock, I quickly grabbed the package and ducked behind some bushes, watching my mother check the empty mailbox. She shut it and then headed toward her uncle's house, confused.

Still in shock, I took off running and jumped over the wall into our next-door neighbor's yard to use their phone. I called home, and Amber answered. I asked for Michelle, and Amber told me she was there too. I quickly explained the phone call and how I had found crack cocaine in the mailbox and taken it. By then, my mom had returned to the house. When she heard it was me on the phone, she realized I had overheard the call and intercepted the package. In the most chilling voice, I heard her say in the background, "Get your ass back here now."

As I scrambled back over the wall, I could hear the shouting. Michelle, Amber, and my mother were all screaming at the top of their lungs. Michelle and Amber were furious; they remembered exactly how things had been the last time our mother was on crack. They started talking about how things had been changing lately and how it all made sense: the money problems, the attitudes, withdrawal, and sleeping for hours on in.

This was the turning point, and I was too ashamed to tell Maya. Instead of opening up, I began acting out in other ways, ultimately leading to me getting kicked out of regular high school and sent to continuation school. After that, tensions between Michelle and my mother escalated until Michelle eventually moved to Las Vegas, leaving only Amber, Jaxon, and me at home with our mom.

As time went on, things continued to deteriorate. My mother began missing work more often, and her appearance changed drastically. She had lost a lot of weight and fell behind on the rent. It was not long before the tension in the house reached an all-time high, with my mother and Amber constantly clashing. Amber was in the 12th grade and pregnant, which my mother shamed her for, while Amber, never one to hold back, would fire right back at her. Their arguments almost always centered on my mother's drug addiction. Soon after Amber gave birth to my first niece, she also moved to Las Vegas.

When Michelle and Amber learned about my mother's relapse, they were understandably furious. They had already endured this nightmare with her once before, and it had left lasting scars. Their emotions shifted between feelings of betrayal, anger, hurt, and disappointment. Since I was too young to remember the daily horrors, we all endured back then, my feelings were different. I was angry, but more than anything, I was hurt and afraid. I felt hurt that we were not enough to keep her grounded and away from drugs. I was also terrified of being taken away again and ending up in another situation like the one we had with Rita and John Wright.

By this time, my mother had already pushed away all the adults who had once been a part of our lives. Her addiction was taking over, and she was too ashamed to face anyone. Jaxon and I found ourselves in a familiar situation. Once again, it was just the two of us left to fend for ourselves. Around the second semester of ninth grade, my mother had fallen so far behind on rent that we had to move. We relocated about 15 minutes outside Pasadena to Highland Park, just outside Los Angeles.

When we moved to Highland Park, my feelings toward my mother shifted. I began to feel angry with her. Though I never outright disrespected her, I lost a lot of respect for her. My mother was a functional addict. She still went to work and paid her bills, but despite managing that, she neglected a major responsibility: her remaining children. Jaxon and I were physically there, but it was as if we didn't exist to her. She would go to work, come home, do her drugs, pace the floor until she fell asleep, and then repeat the cycle the next day. She did not care whether we ate, went to school, or even left the house. Occasionally, she would give us a few dollars to grab snacks from the corner store, which often became our dinner.

Being at home became unbearable and depressing. I started spending more time away just to escape the reality of it all. It hurt me to see her like that. Her body was there, but her mind seemed far away. Whenever she was home, she was high. I can still hear the front door opening and closing at all night hours on the weekends as she makes trips back and forth to her dealer.

At 14, I could not comprehend how someone could function as a person with a substance use disorder. I thought, if she could manage to go to work, maintain her car, and keep a roof over our heads, why couldn't she take care of us? Why weren't we a part of her consciousness? Why did we have to suffer because of her addiction? Now, I realize she needed that job to fuel her habit, her car to get to and from work, and keep a roof over our heads, not necessarily for us, but for her privacy and shelter.

Chapter IX

Continuation School

While at Pasadena High, I got into so much trouble that I developed a bond with the school Dean. I spent so much time in her office. Whether it was for getting kicked out of class, ditching, or fighting, we became close. She was an older Black woman who swiftly became like a grandmother to me. Despite my behavior, I was still a straight-A student during the first semester of ninth grade, and she saw my potential. She believed that with her guidance, she could help me avoid the self-destructive path she saw ahead. Most of the time, when I got into trouble, she would step in and take charge, saying she would handle me. If my offense were not too serious, instead of suspending me and damaging my record, she would assign me to Saturday school or have me participate in school activities. What I saw as punishment, she called redirection.

I remember a time when I was talking to a guy who was the only first-year student on the varsity basketball team. We had been friends before high school due to family connections, and eventually, we started dating, though we never officially labeled it. It was more of an unspoken relationship. One day at lunch, he sat with his teammates, and I heard him telling people we had slept together. I walked up to him and asked if we could talk, but he leaned back, acting cool, and said, "Whatever you have to say to me, you can say in front of my boys." I had this little giggle I would unintentionally do before I got furious. So, I laughed and said, "So you're lying about having sex with me?" He leaned forward, pushed me, and told me to leave. That was the last straw. I climbed onto the table, with him between my legs, and started swinging at his head and face. By the time they pulled me off, he had three big knots across his forehead.

Naturally, I was sent to the Dean's office and expected to be suspended. However, this was one of those times when my "guardian grandmother" stepped in. While disapproving of my actions, she understood my frustrations and chose an alternative punishment. Rumors were circulating that she favored me, and her decision left the head coach furious. He was distraught because one of his varsity players had to miss that evening's game due to the concussion I had given him. Upset, the coach contacted the police, and as a result of the incident, I ended up on house arrest.

Not long after that incident, the Dean retired, and with her gone, I no longer had anyone to step in and save me when I got into trouble. The next time I found myself in that office, I was told, "Your protection is no longer here, and we've had enough; you're expelled." I was in shock. I had been kicked out of Pasadena High School, leaving behind all my friends, or so I thought. Little did I know, several of my friends had also been expelled, and we all ended up at continuation school together.

Rose City High School was a continuation school, also known as an alternative school for students with behavioral issues who struggled in a regular classroom setting. It was game over once I learned my homegirls would be there, too. I knew my life was about to get wild. The school day was only four hours long, so we were out by noon. The classes were small, more like independent studies, and we only had four classes alternating throughout the week. It was literally a cakewalk.

While at Rose City, I managed to keep my grades up, but being there did not help me get back on the right track. It did the opposite. Getting out of school at noon left us with the entire day to do whatever we wanted, which usually meant finding new ways to get into trouble. We were always up to something. At that time, boys were the main focus. Everyone was already sexually active by then, except for me. Honestly, I was that friend who was always around but did not necessarily participate in everything. I'm a Leo, a natural-born leader who doesn't need to follow. Still, I was always down for whatever. We spent our days hopping from house to house and school to school, chasing the next adventure.

When I first started at Rose City, I was in constant trouble. With my mom on drugs and not monitoring me, I had all the freedom I wanted. The only adult I had to answer to was a probation officer, assigned after several run-ins with the law. Apparently, if blood is drawn in a fight, it is considered assault. I had multiple fights that led to assault charges, requiring me to go to court. The first time I was arrested for assault was with an adult; I was fourteen, and she was eighteen. She was Amber's ex-friend who lived across the street. When Amber was pregnant, this girl wanted to fight her, so I intervened because I was not going to allow her to hit Amber while pregnant. I think Amber had confided in her about our family's issues, and when the girl started yelling derogatory things about my mother, I lost control. It was a particularly raw and sensitive time for me. I had a few scuffles in between that required court, but the next big incident was the house arrest situation. At that point, I was appointed court ordered supervision with a probation officer.

Schoolwork was a breeze, and only having to go for half-days made things even easier. That was all my probation officer cared about, and he had no idea what my home life was really like. Most of the time, I wasn't even there; I had started crashing at different friends' houses, only going home to change clothes. Every weekend, you would find me at a house party in the middle of the crowd. We were broke back then, so we'd scrape together a few dollars to give to a guy outside the liquor store to buy us what we could afford: Thunderbird or Cisco with a Kool-Aid packet. I was not into boys or smoking weed yet, but I definitely had my share of alcohol and being out in the streets.

Before I left Pasadena High, I met a boy named Raymond Shields at one of the school pep rallies. We danced our hearts out, each stealing the spotlight from the cheerleaders performing. We cranked up the intensity when we locked our eyes and started battling each other, drawing the entire crowd's attention. From that moment on, a friendship sparked between us. After the rally, we introduced ourselves, and Raymond told me I should try out for a new drill team he was part of. He mentioned it was run by a lady who was actively looking for new girls to join.

I eventually tried out for the drill team, which was a perfect fit. I loved every moment of it. I was never shy about dancing because I was confident in my talent. Tonya Moore, the owner of the drill team, took a real interest in me. She did not just give me a top spot on the team; I had to prove my hard work and dedication. I made it a point to excel at every practice, starting at the back of the line and gradually working my way to the front. The Drill team was a family affair; Tonya was the owner and head of the older girls, her nieces managed the younger girls, and her son Darnell was the head of the drummers. This family was huge and well-known around the city.

As I grew closer to the drill team and its members, I shifted from spending my afternoons on the streets getting into trouble to hanging out with Darnell and his female cousins. Everyone took a liking to me. Darnell became like a big brother, and the rest of the family felt like my own. After school, I would head straight to their grandmother's house, where we would hang out and practice drill team routines until it was time for formal practice.

After months of hanging out and practicing, we got our uniforms. I was too ashamed to admit that my mother would not pay for mine. I missed fittings on purpose, and when those excuses ran out, I finally went for a fitting but was delayed in paying. The most embarrassing part was that one of the drummers, an adult woman who had been my cheer coach in elementary school, had dealt with a similar situation with me. My mother did not want to pay for my uniform back then, so I was taken off the team. I hoped she would not remember or that I could delay things until I found my dad, knowing he would pay for the uniform.

For weeks, I tried reaching my dad without success. I called him so many times and left so many messages that his voicemail was full. I also attempted to contact Grandma Louise to see if she could either ask him to call me back or let me know where he was, but she never answered the phone. I knew what my dad was into, so I assumed he had gotten arrested, and she did not want to tell me.

One morning at school, I received a note from a teacher's aide asking me to come to the front office before we got out at noon. When I arrived, I was told to call home due to an emergency. I reached my mother, who was at home that day, and said she would pick me up to explain everything. Once she picked me up, we drove straight to Los Angeles. During the drive, she informed me that my father had been in a coma for two weeks and that

Grandma Louise wanted to pull the plug, but since I was his power of attorney, I was the only one who could make that decision.

In complete shock, I became hysterical. I could not believe that my mother had picked me up from school to decide to pull the plug on my father, whom I did not even know was ill. There was no empathy or compassion from her. I was also stunned that my grandmother had let him lie there for so long without informing me, his only child. I felt that if my name had not been on his documents, she might have pulled the plug and told me afterward.

When I arrived at the hospital, my dad was lying in the ICU, tubes in his nose and down his throat. I completely lost it to the extent of screaming, crying, and collapsing on the floor. The staff kept picking me up, trying to get me to breathe. A doctor came in and told me that if I did not calm down, they would have to ask me to leave out of respect for the other ICU patients. That snapped me back, and I quickly pulled myself together. I climbed into bed with my dad and laid on his chest. As I lay there, Grandma Louise stood nearby with her usual stern expression, explaining what had happened and urging me to decide to pull the plug. Her words barely registered. I had just found out my dad was here, and she seriously expected me to make that call. She fell silent when she realized I was not listening while my tears soaked in his shirt.

I remember it like it was yesterday. As I lay there, I began saying, "Daddy, please don't leave me. I need you." I just kept repeating it over and over. Suddenly, I felt a jolt. I sat up, and he started choking on the tube in his throat. He opened his eyes and tried to say my name, "Kori." I screamed, but this time, it was out of pure joy. The nurses rushed in, checking his vitals, and removing the tubes. They could not believe it. He was weak but alert and could speak softly, though not in full sentences. He told me he had heard me. He said my cries first got his attention, and then he kept trying to hear my voice. He woke up because he was struggling to hear what I was saying. When I told him, "I said, please don't leave me, I need you," he barely laughed. True to himself, he tried and whispered, "I'm not going anywhere."

Chapter X

Child Abandonment

After everything with my father, Tonya, the owner of the drill team, stepped in and bought my uniform for me. We started competing in competitions and parades almost every other weekend. It became the highlight of my life. I was doing what I loved, and it gave me an escape from my reality while being rewarded at the same time. We often brought home first-place trophies. I never shared what was happening with my mom. So, when people asked why she never came to my performances, I dodged the questions and made excuses.

As my ninth-grade year ended, I had done so well at Rose City that I could return to regular high school after summer break. The catch with Rose City's schedule, having only four classes, was that you had to attend summer school to make up the rest. Instead of returning to Pasadena High, I enrolled in John Muir High School summer classes. Within the first week, a situation with a girl escalated into a fight, though I still do not know why she had an issue with me. Ironically, my probation officer had an office on campus. So, when I was called in after the fight, not only was I kicked out of summer school, but he also wrote me a citation for violating my probation, forcing me to appear in court.

When I was called to court, my biggest fear was not receiving a serious punishment but maybe some community service at worst. My real worry was whether my mother could stay long enough to support me without getting anxious and leaving before we saw the judge. She had done that once before; we left because they took too long to call my name, and I had to face the consequences later.

This time, when I stood before the judge, he looked at me and asked, "What's going on with you? Why are you in my courtroom almost as often as I am?" He asked if everything was okay at home. Of course, I lied and said it was, knowing full well that the moment we left, my mom would head straight home to get high. To anyone who did not know her before the addiction, she just looked skinny, so it was not obvious she was struggling.

The judge then noted that I appeared well taken care of and that, according to my probation officer, I was doing well in school. He could not understand why I kept getting into fights. Then he dropped the bombshell: "Today is Friday. I am going to send you to juvenile detention for the weekend so you can see this is not the path you want to take in life. Your mother can pick you up Sunday afternoon."

As the bailiff approached and motioned for me to walk around the bench, I fell apart. I was crying, pleading, swearing I would not be back, and insisting I did not need to experience jail to learn my lesson. But none of that mattered. I was definitely heading to the juvenile hall for the weekend. Once I was processed in, I was allowed to use the phone to call my mom collect. She accepted the call and told me I had brought this on myself, but I would be fine. It was just two days. I spent all of Saturday listening to the other girls' stories and felt relieved knowing I had only 24 hours left. Since the calls were collect and expensive, I waited until Saturday evening to call my mom again to remind her to pick me up the next day. She assured me she would be there. Sunday afternoon came and went. The designated window for pickups closed, and then the units were locked down. My mom never showed up.

I had to wait until Monday morning to call her again. I dialed repeatedly, but no one answered. Finally, in the late afternoon, Jaxon picked up. When I asked where Mom was, he told me she had gone to work. I did not believe him; there was no way she was at work. I was sure she was on her way to pick me up. As the hours passed and she still did not show, I became anxious and called home again. This time, my mom answered. She told me she had to go to work and could not miss any more time because of me. When I asked if she would be coming the next day, she responded, "I'll see." I broke down, crying and pleading with her to please come get me. The next day came, and again, she did not show. I called and called, and when I finally spoke to her on Tuesday evening, I begged her to come. She hung up the phone on me.

By the third day past my weekend sentence, I tried calling home again, only to discover that the phone was now blocked from receiving collect calls. Panic set in; I could not get through anymore. I only knew a few landline numbers, but none of them accepted collect calls. Back then, it was an extra feature most people did not have. Realizing my mother was not coming to get me, I told the staff I was not supposed to be there. Every day, I repeated myself, but no one took me seriously. Instead, they just made sarcastic comments like, "No one's supposed to be here," or "Everyone's innocent." They were teasing me rather than helping.

When I first arrived at the detention center, the nurse conducted a full physical. During the exam, I mentioned that I had asthma. As a result, she placed a colored wristband on me, indicating to the staff that I was exempt from being pepper-sprayed and that they would need to use alternative methods of restraint if I ever became aggressive. As the days turned into weeks and then months, I felt increasingly helpless and frustrated. Every morning at 5 a.m., just before the 6 a.m. wake-up call, the guards would come by to collect anyone with a court appearance that day. They would be taken to eat first before being transported to the courthouse. Each night, I would pray that the next morning would be my turn. I would wake up before 5 a.m., hoping the guard would stop at my door. But I would tear up whenever I heard those keys pass me by. I would lie there repeating to myself, "I just need one person to believe me; just one." As I lay there, night after night, I vowed that if I were ever in a position to help someone, I would because sometimes all it takes is one person to make a difference.

Knowing the staff could not use pepper spray on me, I pushed boundaries more. Whenever I asked for help and was dismissed, I would lash out, attacking the staff, spitting at them, and becoming increasingly aggressive as my anger and sense of abandonment grew. They began stripping away my privileges, like dayroom time and phone calls, even though I had no one to call. Still, I made sure to settle down just enough on Sundays to attend chapel for church. In those moments, I felt like being in the house of the Lord would help Him hear my prayers more clearly.

One day, there was a staff member whose name I cannot recall and whose face is a blur now, but she decided to sit down and talk to me while I was in the dayroom. She bluntly asked, "Why are you always showing your ass?" And before I could respond, she followed up with, "When's your next court date?" I answered both questions, saying, "I act out because I don't have a court date, and I'm not even supposed to be here, but nobody will listen to me." She then asked how I knew I did not have a court date, and I explained, "I came here for a weekend stay, but my mom never came to pick me up."

She looked me straight in the eyes and said, "Look at me, I'm a big woman. We do not have access to your records in this building; we only have a file we update. The distance to the records office is no walk in the park. But if I go over there and find out you are lying, there will be consequences. Still, I will do this for you because you've been persistent, and now your behavior is getting out of hand."

When she returned, her eyes were filled with tears. She first said, "I am so sorry, baby." My weekend order was just a few sheets of paper instead of a full case file, so somehow, it got buried under other documents, and I had essentially been lost in the system. No one noticed the mistake because my mother never came for me. There was no actual case pending. I was only supposed to stay for two days, but it had turned into three months. Once this became known, they rushed to get me out of there. An emergency hearing was held, and my mother lost custody for child abandonment, making me a ward of the state once again.

Not wanting to keep me in detention any longer, I was sent to a group home while the courts searched for a foster placement. At the group home, I had access to a house phone that let me call cell phones, something I could not do from the pay phone at the detention center. The first person I tried to call was my dad, but his number was disconnected, leaving me with no way to reach him. The feeling of being in the same city as my father and not being able to talk or see him was devastating. Whenever we left the group home for any reason, my head was on a swivel because I knew I was not too far from my dad and could run into him. The next number I remembered was Darnell's. As I called him, hearing his voice felt like a lifeline. He had been there at my last fight before everything spiraled, but he did not know what had happened since he had not seen or heard from me. Tonya jumped into action when I explained everything to him and his mom. She had an aunt who was a licensed foster parent, and with no children in her home at the time, Tonya immediately started making calls to help.

Chapter XI

Foster Care 2.0

I'm not sure how Tonya did it, but she pulled some strings, and she and Darnell were able to visit me at the group home for my 15th birthday. I was beyond excited to see them because I had not seen a familiar face in months. Though the visit was brief, it was the perfect birthday surprise. That evening, I spent the rest of my birthday lying in bed, staring up at the ceiling, listening to the oldies on 92.3 The Beat. During all of this, I still had not spoken to my mother since she hung up on me three months earlier. Within a few weeks, Tonya had arranged for me to be placed in her aunt's foster care.

Driving down the 110 Freeway, leaving Los Angeles, and heading toward Pasadena, I felt incredible relief. I was moving in with Tonya's Aunt

Judy and her husband, Pastor Williams, who lived just a short walk from John Muir. It was so refreshing to be back in familiar territory. When I arrived at their home, Aunt Judy and Pastor Williams greeted me warmly, welcoming me with open arms. They showed me to the room I would be staying in and only asked that I be respectful, stay on top of my studies, and attend church every Sunday morning. I could tell right away this was going to be a different experience from the first time I was in foster care.

The first thing we did was get me enrolled in school. At Muir, they were skeptical about accepting me because of my prior record. I had only attended summer school there for 3 days before I was kicked out for fighting. After explaining my situation, they gave me a second chance and let me enroll. This was the start of my new normal. I was in a stable environment, had adult supervision, and was held accountable for everything I did. My life had seemed to be getting back on track.

Shortly after enrolling in school, Aunt Judy took me to the dentist for a routine cleaning. I was not experiencing any tooth pain, and my teeth appeared to be in good shape; there was no plaque buildup, and I'd never had any cavities before. As a ward of the court, I was provided with health and dental insurance. Looking back, I am convinced they filled all my side and back teeth with silver fillings during that dentist visit just to bill the insurance.

A few weeks later, I had a physical exam and my first pap smear. Although I was not sexually active, my menstrual cycles were irregular. The doctor discovered a small cyst on my ovaries, which was harmless and likely to dissolve on its own. While the cyst eventually went away, I was also told during that visit that I would not be able to have children. I was unsure how to react since having kids was far from my mind at that point. I accepted the news and moved on.

While staying with Aunt Judy, I was aware that, as a ward of the state, she received money for having me there. I am not sure how much she got, but whenever the payment came through, she would place a stack of about three hundred one-dollar bills on my dresser. I figured the check went straight into her bank account, and she gave me the ones from the church offering plate. Regardless, I appreciated every dollar. It gave me a sense of responsibility and taught me the basics of managing money.

Things were really starting to turn around for me. I was staying out of trouble, reconnected with my dad, and got back into competing with the drill team. I did not think much of it then, but looking back, I realized that my dad was noticeably absent whenever legal issues arise. Yet, he always seemed to reappear once everything had calmed down. I was not in touch with any of my other relatives; Michelle and Amber were still in Las Vegas. I only remember speaking to my grandmother around the holidays, and my mom and Jaxon were not too far away, but that situation was what it was.

Since Tonya was part of the family, it was only natural that Aunt Judy allowed me to spend much time with her. Their family had pretty much adopted me. Eventually, it became so frequent that I sometimes stayed overnight during the week. Aunt Judy did not seem to mind until I started missing church. For some reason, every Sunday, I would wake up feeling sick and unable to attend, or I would stay the night with Tonya and skip church the next morning. Aunt Judy eventually warned me that if I kept missing church, I would not be able to hang out with Tonya as much.

At first, everything was all good; I had gotten used to the money Aunt Judy was giving me. I was able to buy new clothes and shoes more often than I had ever before. I became addicted to fashion. I started doing hair on the side to make extra money just so that I could shop. After school, I always had a head to do; if you were a guy with braids during that time nine times out of ten, I did them. I was good; I did designs and had what people called growing hands. If I didn't have a weekend competition, I was either doing individual braids or sew-in weave. Sometimes, depending on the style, I could knock out two or three heads a day, bringing in the cash.

School life was great, and being at Muir was a completely different experience from Pasadena High. Muir was more focused on sports and fashion, with the popular kids standing out, while Pasadena High leaned more toward academics. Half of the girls on the drill team also went to Muir, so we spent time together both during and after school and performed on the weekends. The drill team was like a symbol of our city; when we competed, we represented Pasadena. What started as something that felt like a family affair slowly evolved into more of a clique, almost like a gang, though not to that extreme.

In other cities, our competitors embraced and welcomed us, and with our long-standing first-place winning streak, our team became a fan favorite. However, within our own city, we faced more conflict and animosity. Some drill team members grew unhappy with how things were being run and decided to leave, forming their own team. At first, the tension between the team owners was minor, but it gradually escalated and affected us kids as well. Since some of us went to the same school, there would be back-and-forth banter between us. We practiced in the front yard on Raymond Ave on specific days, and coincidentally, the owner of the new team lived on the same block and held practice on the same days. It turned into a kind of battle of the drums during practice sessions.

Things quickly escalated. Accusations of copying routines started flying, comparisons between the kids became frequent, and members began switching between teams, spreading rumors on both sides. Eventually, tensions reached a boiling point, and things turned physical. Sometimes, it was a one-on-one fight, while other times, entire teams clashed against each other. During these brawls, everybody was expected to be swinging. Instead of things calming down as time went on, it seemed like every week, the brawls got bigger. Because Pasadena is relatively small, somehow everybody is related to everybody, so the beef between the teams spilled over to other family members.

Growing up, I was more of a lover than a fighter. I preferred laughing and having fun over being angry or upset; bad moods never stuck with me for long. But my attitude shifted when I watched my mother lose everything, bit by bit. That made me so angry inside. I never took it out on her, never confronted her, or demanded an apology; I just bottled it up and unleashed it on everyone else. When I moved in with Aunt Judy, I started feeling like my old self again, like I had no reason to be mad because my life had regained some stability. The only problem was I had already earned a reputation as a good fighter by then.

Aunt Judy had no idea that I was heavily involved in the chaos. She had no clue about all the fights I was getting into, and I am certain that if she had known, she would have pulled me off the team, family or not. During the height of the drill team drama, I was completely out of control, fighting anyone who crossed my path: girls my age, grown women, and even a peer's grandmother. At that point, I did not care. I was not fighting for any personal reason; I was just caught up in madness and fought because I was there and most definitely expected to.

While I was staying with Aunt Judy during 10th grade, it was the only year in high school when I could participate in school activities. That year, I attended Homecoming for both Muir and Pasadena High. Before and after that, I missed out on everything. In ninth grade, my mother could not afford me to attend any events, so I missed those memories. After I left Aunt Judy's, I was pretty much on my own and could not afford it either.

10th grade was also the only year in high school when I had a boyfriend—my first real relationship. With no clear title, the situation I mentioned earlier never went beyond the friend zone; he had moved on to someone else. But this relationship was different; it was official, and we were inseparable. Every school morning, he would catch the bus to my house so we could walk to school together. Once a week, he had put twenty dollars on my Nextel chirp phone, which was basically him paying my bill. We shared a locker, and during every passing period, we would meet up there just to see each other. As far as we were concerned, we were in love. We used to skip our last class of the day, both of which were easy-to-pass electives, just to sit across the street and kiss until the final bell rang. We would talk on the phone for hours at night until one of us eventually fell asleep.

Not long after the school year ended, maybe a week or two into summer break, my world shifted again. I had just turned sixteen, and while I cannot recall the details, I vaguely remember hearing that the money Aunt Judy was receiving for me either stopped or was reduced because of my age. Regardless, Aunt Judy was not willing to handle the financial change. I do not remember exactly how Aunt Judy told me I had to leave, but I do remember feeling scared. I did not want to uproot and move in with another foster family. I was afraid of the possibility of being sent far away or, worse, not finding a home at all and ending up in another group home.

Back then, I wasn't so much angry as I was deeply hurt by Aunt Judy's decision to let me go. It hurt because we had built a close bond. Even though I spent much time with Tonya, Aunt Judy and I shared special moments going out to eat, shopping, and running errands. In the mornings before school, we would sit at the table and have oatmeal and toast before starting our day. She taught me little things I will never forget, like properly placing the tissue on the roller. As a child, I felt like I should have been worth more than just a check. Aunt Judy had briefly made my life better, only for it to feel like it was being taken away again.

Leaving her home brought back the same frustration I had felt with my mother. When I was reunited with my mom after foster care, I did everything I could to be a child worth fighting for, hoping it would keep her from returning to drugs. But it did not work; I felt like I was not enough. Now, with Aunt Judy, even after I turned my life around and got back on the right path, money became the deciding factor, rather than my growth or who I was as a person being enough.

Chapter XII

The Moore Family

Scared and uncertain, I had no idea what would happen after leaving Aunt Judy's house. My mother had left the house in Highland Park and moved back to Pasadena, living in a two-bedroom apartment on Fair Oaks with Jaxon. She was still using drugs and had taken a leave of absence from her job. With no work to occupy her time, she was getting high more often, sinking deeper into her addiction.

By the grace of God, I did not end up back with my mother or in another foster home. Once again, Tonya stepped in and offered me a place to stay. Besides her only child, Darnell, she had also taken in one of her great-nephews and another kid from the drill team who was having issues at home. Tonya was a young mother, but she took care of business. She had a full-time job, ran the drill team, and still had a social life.

Living in a house with three boys who became like brothers was challenging. Darnell was the oldest, then me; Aaron was a year younger, and Cameron, the youngest, was ten. They would constantly play tricks on me and mess with me for no reason. Sometimes, it was all in good fun, but it really got on my nerves other times. Darnell did not mess with me much, but he would laugh hysterically when the others did.

Tonya was like a sour patch. Sometimes, she is sour, sometimes sweet, and she can be intimidating. She was one of four sisters, not the oldest but the most outspoken and in charge. Tonya had a magnetic personality that drew people in because she was fun and loving, with a tough exterior that hid her soft heart. I think she talked a lot of smack, mostly because she enjoyed it, and it helped keep everyone in line.

Living with Tonya kept me on my toes. Like most Black mothers, she was up bright and early every Saturday morning for chores. What I never understood, though, was why she would wake us up yelling like the house had turned upside down overnight. Her place was always tidy; no dishes were in the sink, and the bedrooms and bathrooms were always in order. Our chores were simple and routine: doing laundry, wiping down the bathroom, and tidying up the living room. But she would be going off like we were living in filth, acting as if there were rats and roaches everywhere.

When I moved in with Tonya, she did not receive any supplemental income for taking me in, which meant I was just an extra mouth to feed. She never made me feel bad about it, but at 16, I knew I had to find a way to contribute so I would not be a burden. I understood that taking me in was already a big responsibility, so I did everything I could to avoid giving her a reason to change her mind. I walked on eggshells daily because I was terrified of being put out.

Tonya's family was large, with many nieces, nephews, and cousins who mostly hung out at her mom's house, known to everyone as BigMa. The whole family embraced me, and I became one of them. Tonya's nieces became my cousins, and we were all tight knit. My only fear was getting into it with any of them because if you clash with one, you had to deal with them all. Initially, I was always nervous because everyone had such short tempers. The vibe was always that you were either with us or against us. I chose to be with them very early on, meaning I did whatever they were doing. I could not afford not to. I had nowhere else to go.

Just when I thought I was on the right track, everything shifted once more in the world of Kori. I grew closer to the Moore family, and soon we became inseparable. Their friends became my friends, and their enemies became mine. Wherever we went, conflicts seemed to follow, often escalating into brawls. Not all the grudges were rooted in the Moores' affairs; I had my own disputes, too, but they always had my back, just as I had theirs.

Things had gotten so bad around the city that I could no longer go anywhere. I had to be picked up and dropped off at school, and I could not even go to the store alone. Someone always had to be with me. I remember one time when Tonya's niece and I were at a party, and she started arguing with a guy who was well over 6'5". As the argument escalated, he positioned himself like he was about to hit her. I was standing on the stairs, level with his head, and before he could make a move, I swung and hit him in the temple, knocking him out cold.

When he came to, he was furious, looking around to see who had done it. When everyone pointed at me, he came after me. I bolted into the street and got clipped by a car, but I managed to stay on my feet and kept running. I got away that night, but I knew like hell it was far from over. That is one thing about living in a small city: the beef is never over until it is over. Not long after, I disobeyed orders to never leave the house alone. I had been waiting all day for my brothers to return so we could go to the store, but I eventually decided to go on my own since it was only a block away. When I turned the corner, I saw the huge guy I had knocked out coming down the street on a bike. As soon as he saw me, he jumped off his bike, still rolling, planted his feet, and pulled up his pants, ready to fight. I knew he would rock my world in the worst way because I had embarrassed him in front of his boys and others. Just in the nick of time, my brothers came around the corner, and before the car was even in park, two of them had already jumped out.

I felt so relieved, but I knew I was in for a world of trouble.

Over time, I became a real problem. My behavior was never an issue for the Moore family, though. They thrived on drama; whether it annoyed or made them laugh hysterically, they lived for it. On top of the daily fights, the more time I spent with my adoptive cousins, the more I picked up the habit of shoplifting. At the time, I did not see myself as a thief; I thought of it as survival. I had never needed to steal before, but after moving in with Tonya, who was not receiving financial help for me, I often had to fend for myself. I stole all my hygiene products and toiletries from grocery stores, so I would not burden Tonya with buying them. There were many times when I already felt like a burden, so I did not ask for much.

I felt that Tonya and her family had already done more than enough for me by taking me in. At that moment, I was forever in their debt. I was willing to do whatever it took to show my loyalty to the family, especially since mine had disappeared. With nowhere else to turn, if I had to fight, steal, swindle, or hustle to fit in, I did it. Sometimes, I wished my situation were different, but while living with Tonya, I never really got to experience my high school years the way I had hoped.

Tonya was still young and enjoying life. She spent her time going out and hanging at motorcycle clubs. She did not really care whether I went to school or not as long as I didn't end up at the police station again like I had so many times before. While she was out with her friends, I used one of Darnell's friend's spare IDs to go out with the older cousins. I started going to 21-and-over clubs at 16. I had no business being there, but with no real supervision, I could pretty much do whatever I wanted. I was having fun at the moment, but deep down, I would have much rather been at homecoming or school dances with my friends.

The one time I ever got to go to homecoming during high school was when I lived with Aunt Judy. Other than that, something always came up, and I never pushed the issue because of my situation. During prom season, we even went to get me fitted for a custom dress, but then my youngest adoptive brother got into serious trouble, and all attention shifted to him. I understood what was important then, and prom was not a priority. I never got to go to prom either, but I was able to braid enough hair to get my ticket to grad night.

Living with Tonya forced me to grow up quickly. I was essentially an adult in a minor's body. I had to figure out how to survive, make money, get what I needed, and keep up my grades. Through it all, I focused on one goal: walking across the stage to receive my diploma. No matter what was happening outside of school or at home, my determination to graduate never wavered.

Chapter XIII

Small World

In a world where they say there are six degrees of separation, there are more like two in Pasadena, CA. Everyone knows or is related to someone. Even though I moved over the summer after 10th grade, my boyfriend and I were still going strong. I had only moved 20 minutes away across the freeway but spent most of my time in Pasadena. We would often meet up and hang out at the park near his house in Altadena, a suburb of Pasadena separated by just one street. Altadena is known for being protected by a Crip-affiliated gang, while Pasadena is mostly Blood-affiliated, with some Hispanic gangs mixed in. Since Altadena did not have a high school, all the kids had to cross over into Blood territory to attend school. I never saw that as a problem, thinking kids were off-limits unless they chose to get involved in gang life.

After summer ended and we returned to school, I found myself caught up in yet another conflict with a different group of girls. They were not even students at my school this time, they were middle and high school dropouts, heavily involved in street life. These six girls, aged 17 to 19, were identified as gang members from one of Pasadena's Blood gangs. Their issue with me stemmed from the fact that I grew up around and hung out with Bloods but was dating someone and spending time in Crip territory. I did not think it mattered, especially since neither my boyfriend nor I were involved with either gang.

Somehow, I became their target, and the harassment started. These girls would drive by after school and throw rocks, water bottles, whatever they had out of the car. They never stopped or got out since I was always at the bus stop on school property. I did not know them personally, but I knew of them, and they knew of me and my reputation. I had never been one to shy away from a fight or lose one. With the confidence that I could handle myself, my mouth was just as bold as my fists.

One day after school, a friend asked me to walk to McDonald's with her. I initially said no because I needed to take the bus home and remove my braids. She suggested I catch the bus from the stop near McDonald's, and I agreed, thinking I could grab something to eat since I was hungry. As we entered the McDonald's parking lot, I glanced back toward the street, and sure enough, I locked eyes with every girl in that car. Within seconds, I saw their brake lights come on, and the car began to make a U-turn. At that moment, I knew things were about to go down. I just kept walking and got in line to order food.

While my friend and I stood in line, I saw the girls exiting their car and heading inside. I turned to my friend and said, "Oh, here we go," knowing things would escalate. I knew myself well enough to realize I would not back down, even though I was outnumbered. As all six of them surrounded me, the ringleader spoke up first, saying, "I heard you be up there on the Flock," using a term meant to disrespect the Altadena Block Crips. Being who I am, I responded, "I don't know about all that, but if you mean the Block, then yeah." She laughed out of frustration and started making threats. Of course, I could not hold my tongue and said, "I'm not scared of any of you Slob-ass bitches," using the ultimate insult against their gang. That is when the punches started flying.

At first, I was holding my own, mixing it up with the first girl, but then the others jumped in, and soon it was six against one. At some point, I fell between the tables, and instead of hitting me, they started ripping out my braids. The center of my hair was braided in a beehive, while the perimeter was done in individuals. By the time they were finished, I had only three braids left and was almost completely bald. Out of everyone in the crowded restaurant, the only person who came to my defense was the brother of one of my friends, who was also affiliated with the same gang as the girls. He started throwing them off me, while the girl I came with didn't even help.

After the fight ended, the girls ran out, jumped into their car, and sped off. By then, so many people had already called Tonya and Darnell that they were on their way. While trying to catch my breath, I saw the friend I had come to McDonald's walking up to the counter and grabbing a bag of food. I knew we had not ordered anything before the fight started, so I was confused about how she managed to get food while I was getting jumped. I flew into a rage before she could even reach into the bag. I grabbed her by the neck and tossed her over the counter, ready to do her in the worst way. After all, I was only there because she asked me, and she did nothing to help.

Once everybody got me off of her and peeled her off the floor, Tonya, Darnell, and a few others pulled up. To say they were pissed is an extreme understatement. When Tonya saw me and my hair, she yelled, "Get in the car now!" She was yelling so loud and fast in the car that I barely understood her the whole time. Instead of going home, she drove to the girls' hangout spot. You could see them in the front yard, reenacting the fight as we pulled up. When Tonya got out of the car, she told them, "All you bitches line it up; she needs her fair one." They all knew and respected Tonya, so they started to plead their case, calling Tonya OG and telling her I said this and that. Tonya was not hearing it and told them they knew they could not fight me one-on-one.

Naturally, the biggest and worst one stepped into the street first. We squared up and started throwing punches, and I was getting the upper hand. At one point, I grabbed her head and slammed it into a parked car, leaving a dent. She bounced off the car and sent me tumbling to the ground against a tree. She gained the upper hand by sitting on me and landed a few too many punches to my face, and I did not take hits well. With every ounce of strength I had, I managed to lift her off me, giving us enough space to stand. Then I hit her with a combo that sent her straight to the ground; she was snoring before she even hit the pavement. With my adrenaline pumping, I screamed out, "Who's next?" But no one else wanted to fight. I was tired, but I vowed to each of them that I would catch them one-on-one one day and would not be nice about it.

After that entire ordeal, I had to lay low regarding fighting. The perimeter of my hair was completely bald, but thankfully, the middle was still protected, and I had a decent length left. I had to either flat iron my hair or style it in a deep swoop to cover up the hair loss.

My boyfriend and I were still very much in love at that time. I knew he lived with his grandparents, but he never really explained why. Whatever he shared was enough for me to stop asking questions. It was always with such admiration that whenever he talked about his mother, he never criticized or spoke poorly about her. In fact, he referred to her as his best friend, saying they could talk about anything. You could hear the love in his tone when he mentioned her.

One day, while we were sitting in our usual spot by the school, an old, beat-up car that was smoking and making all sorts of noise pulled up beside us. The look on his face was one of shock, as if he had seen a ghost. The lady rolled down the window and said, "Hey, mama's baby." It turned out to be his mother, and he was clearly embarrassed, as it was evident she was struggling with some drug addiction. He had never mentioned this before; he did not want me to know that his mother had a substance abuse problem.

Unbeknownst to him, I was hiding a similar secret about my own mother. He thought I had been court-ordered to leave home because of my behavior. The rest of that afternoon felt awkward; I think we cut our hangout short and went our separate ways. Later that night, while we were on the phone, I could still hear the embarrassment in his voice. I decided to share the truth about my mother to address the elephant in the room. I told him how my life had felt like it flashed before my eyes and how everything and everyone I once knew, as my family and my world, were gone, all because my mom had relapsed into drug use.

Talking about our truths ultimately brought us closer. It felt like we both understood what the other was going through and could relate in a way no one else could. Neither of us had shared anything about our mothers; it felt like we were silently enduring our struggles alone. My mother had moved not far from our high school, so some days, we would skip school and hang out at her apartment. Most of the time, she would be there, but so high that she did not even realize we were not in school. As teenagers wanting to be together all the time, we took advantage of my mother's oblivion to what was happening around her. Sometimes, we would have Jaxon leave the door unlocked so we could sneak in and spend the night. I remember lying on the living room floor while my mother walked past us at least four times without noticing we were there. Granted, it was dark, but she was so high and lost in her own world that she never noticed.

One evening, my boyfriend and I were at my mother's apartment when she came home. I cannot remember where she had been, but I knew she was not high and seemed to be in her normal state. It felt nice to see her like that for a change. Not long after she got out of her street clothes, there was a knock at the door. My mother was in the back, and my boyfriend and I were in the living room. I glanced out the window next to the door and saw a man I recognized from before. Before opening the door, I looked at my boyfriend, rolled my eyes, and said, "Of course, it's her dealer." He and my boyfriend exchanged glances when I opened the door, and he stepped inside. The man called my boyfriend by name and asked what he was doing there. To my surprise, my mother's drug dealer turned out to be my boyfriend's sister's dad and his mother's boyfriend. What a small world, right?

The coincidence was unfortunate and left my boyfriend feeling ashamed, as if his family were somehow contributing to the issues in mine. He seemed to think he had some connection to his mother and her boyfriend using drugs with my mother. This situation created a bit of distance between us. Meanwhile, now that everyone was acquainted, his younger sister loved me, and his mother adored me, which brought us closer together. However, the more I bonded with the side of his family he wanted to keep hidden, the further apart we grew. Eventually, he began cheating on me with a girl I was friendly with at school, and we ended up breaking up and going our separate ways.

I struggled with the breakup because he was the first person I connected with on such a personal level. He knew things about me that even Maya did not know. Although our journeys were different, we shared a similar story. We both felt the same hurt and betrayal from our parents and leaned on each other for motivation when we were feeling low. Losing that support during such a vulnerable time was incredibly difficult for me. I was always surrounded by people but still felt alone because no one knew me the way he did.

Chapter XIV

Class of '05

During the first semester of my senior year, I was still attending John Muir High School. I kept up my grades from 10th grade through senior year, looking forward to graduation. About halfway through the semester, seniors who were missing credits and off track for graduation were called into the office. To my surprise, I was among them. It turned out I had missed credits from ninth grade that I had not completed because I was expelled from summer school during my transition from Rose City. I had completely forgotten about the two classes I missed. At Muir, my only option was to complete summer classes to receive my diploma. This was unacceptable to me. I had to walk across the stage with my graduating class.

Pasadena High School was the first school I attended, and I knew they offered a program designed to help students catch up on past classes at their own pace while keeping up with their current coursework. It was primarily for pregnant students or those trying to get back on track for graduation. I realized that if I transferred back to Pasadena High, I could still walk across the stage with all of my friends, including Maya and Tylan. All I needed was a guardian to complete a transfer form, allowing one school to release me and the other to accept me.

Unfortunately, at the time, I did not have a guardian who was fully invested in helping me graduate on time. I was living with Tonya, but she worked during the day. When I told her about my situation, she said she could not take time off to go to school, so I would need to figure something else out. Out of desperation, I even asked my mother for help, but she could not assist me then. Eventually, I got tired of waiting and not progressing toward my credits. I do not remember exactly how, but I forged the paperwork on both ends, successfully getting me where I needed to be.

For the next few months, I stayed home and worked on two ninth-grade classes and four of my current senior classes. I would study for 72-hour stretches, pausing only to eat and shower. After each session, I would rest my hands and eyes for a day before starting another 72-hour session. About five weeks in, I developed a cyst on my wrist from all the writing. At that time, all our assignments were still handwritten from textbooks, and we had to read for answers. Eventually, I had to go to the doctor to have the cyst drained.

After months of relentless effort, I finally caught up on all my missing credits and even finished my senior classes early. Two months before the school year ended, I had earned all my credits and secured my place on the 2005 graduating class list. When I stood in the school office and received the news, it was just the dean, the principal, the program instructor, and me. When I heard the words "congratulations" leave her lips, my body weakened, and I collapsed to the floor. Tears streamed down my face, yet the room remained completely silent. At that moment, I think everyone understood that my reaction reflected the immense effort it took for me to reach that point.

Until that point, every effort I made in life seemed either unnoticed or never enough. In elementary school, while living at the Wright home, I excelled academically and followed all the rules at home, but it did not stop the physical abuse. When I was with my mother, striving to be her shining star only ended with me being left at a detention center and becoming a ward of the state. With Aunt Judy, money overshadowed my growth and stability, while living with Tonya felt like walking on a fragile glass floor, forcing me to tread carefully.

I think graduating was the one achievement no one could downplay or take away from me. It is something that I can keep and will follow me wherever I go. It was a goal I set for myself and a gift I wanted to give to my mother. None of my siblings had graduated from high school, and I wanted to be the one she could watch walking across the stage. Despite everything we had been through, I still wanted to give her that moment.

I was incredibly proud of myself for fighting tooth and nail to finish school. During my high school years, I faced my mother's relapse, my sisters moving away, losing our home, constant fighting, house arrest, juvenile hall, continuation school, and foster care. Along the way, I got caught up in partying, drinking, and stealing, yet I still managed to stay focused on what I needed to do. The morning of graduation rehearsal, I had been out all night at a twenty-one and older club, and when I showed up to practice, I was so hungover that Maya brought me coffee while Tylan brought me tea. My actions were irresponsible, but my priorities remained intact.

Many people were surprised to see me in a white and red cap and gown on the morning of graduation. They had assumed I was still attending John Muir, whose colors were blue and gold. I dropped the news that I had switched schools to make this day possible. Each student was given ten tickets, and the ceremony was held at the Rose Bowl Stadium. That day, I felt the support of over twenty people who came to cheer me on, including my mother. I was thrilled—this was the moment I had been waiting for, especially after Michelle and Amber dropped out.

The graduating class was large, probably over 250, but fewer than 300 students. With my last name beginning with a W, my name was called near the end. Looking out from the stage, I realized my mother was no longer in the audience. After the ceremony, I asked where my mother was when we flipped our caps and gathered with our families. My grandmother simply said, "You know your mother can't sit still long enough without needing a fix." At that moment, I realized she had left before seeing me walk across the stage.

It felt like a huge slap in the face. That was another one of my efforts that was not enough for her to sit still for just two hours. At that moment, I thought I had literally handed my mother a proud moment, and she left to smoke drugs. I started feeling like she would never choose me. Before, I thought no matter what I did, she always favored my sisters over me, and now that they were not around, she was choosing drugs over me. I struggled with this realization, but it never stopped me from wanting to make her proud.

Chapter XV

Eighteen is not grown

A few months after graduation, I turned eighteen and started working at a Bank of America call center that summer. I needed my birth certificate to apply, but I had no idea where the original was. I had asked my mother and grandmother about it years before, but neither of them had it. So, I went to the records office and ordered a new one. When I received it, I noticed a name listed as my father that was not my father. Without hesitation, I called my mother. She had no idea I had been searching for my birth certificate or that I had ordered a new one. When she answered, I asked first, "Who is John Doe?" Without missing a beat or showing any confusion, she replied, "Oh, that's a name I made up for your birth certificate when I was mad at your dad." It was a big shock by how extreme that was; I just said, "Okay." It struck

154

me as odd that she remembered a name she had invented 18 years ago, especially since she had not seen the document in about 10 years but recalled it without hesitation.

Bank of America was my first real job, and looking back, it is funny now, but at the time, I was so embarrassed when I asked when summer break started. I was the youngest person on the team, possibly in the entire building, and it was obvious. The older woman just laughed and said, "Have you ever seen your mother or any other adult take the summer off?" I laughed along, but it was out of pure embarrassment.

During the summer, while working at the call center, I prepared for the upcoming fall semester at the local community college, Pasadena City College (PCC). It was where everyone who did not get into or attend a university ended up. Even though I had worked hard in school, caught up on my credits, and graduated as part of the Honors Society with a GPA good enough for a university, I lacked the support and guidance to take that next step. I am sure I could have gone to a counselor for help, but then what? My home life did not provide the

155

resources or knowledge about what colleges were looking for or how to make my application stand out. All I knew was that I needed a good GPA. The only community service I had done was court-ordered. We did not have those types of conversations at home. Most of the people around me were on welfare, getting food stamps, or collecting disability checks for their children.

Enrolling in school was quite challenging. Every step seemed to come with a roadblock. First, there was the application, which was the most tedious thing I had ever filled out, and I had no idea how to complete the sections asking for parental information. I initially took the paperwork to my mother, hoping she could help, but her income disqualified me from receiving financial aid. It was absurd to me. How could she not qualify when she was currently on leave, caught up in an extended drug binge? The irony was that, despite her chaotic life, she appeared to be an average middle-class citizen on paper. My other option was to take out a loan with her as a co-signer, but she refused. My father had no documented income, and since he was not listed on my birth certificate, that option was a dead end, too.

When I could not qualify for financial aid through my parents, I discovered that being a former state ward could make me automatically eligible. At 18, still learning how to navigate these things, I started making phone calls and sending request forms, but nothing came of it. I did not really know where to begin, so I just called courthouses in areas where I had been at some point. Eventually, I gave up on financial aid and decided to try again when I turned twenty-one and could apply independently. In the meantime, I took on a second job at Banana Republic to help pay for my classes.

Starting at PCC was a great experience. Maya, my cousin Shannon, and her friends, who had graduated the year before, were there. It felt like a completely different world. I met new people and reconnected with old friends. Over time, Shannon and I started hanging out more. She was living with her dad full-time, and I would stay over at their place most nights. Our schedules were almost identical. We both worked near the college and had similar class times. After long work and school days, we would spend the nights partying hard. We were part of a group that hung out at a house near the school, and we would get "white boy wasted," only to wake up and do it all over again.

Eventually, the excitement of starting college wore off. I gained the typical "freshman 15," and when grades came out, reality hit hard; I failed every class. Life had completely overwhelmed me. I worked two jobs to pay for classes I could barely stay awake in. I did not give up immediately; I tried to refocus and turn things around. I was technically still living with Tonya then, but I spent most nights either with Shannon or at the hangout spot with our crew. Tonya got fed up with me constantly coming and going, and one day, she said, "Obviously, you have somewhere to live, so you can stop running in and out of my house." Her timing could not have been worse.

My relationship with my dad was more like that of my siblings. We would have our falling outs and go our separate ways until one of us eventually gave in. I was a brat most of the time, but he had his moments of pettiness, too. When Tonya asked me to leave, my dad and I were not speaking, so I went to stay with Shannon and her father. I was still working and going to school, but I was a little more focused. Shannon had a car, so I often just tagged along with her, doing whatever she was doing. By then, she was in her second year of college and had already figured out how to balance school, work, and her social life.

When the tax season arrived, I was determined to buy myself a car. It was my first time filing taxes, and I was ready to step into adulthood and handle things independently. I was also in the middle of a disagreement with my dad and wanted to prove I could do something on my own. But, as always, drama found its way in. When I filed my taxes, they were garnished because of back taxes owed from 1992. I was five years old in 1992, clearly not working or filing taxes, but the IRS was not concerned with that. I had to spend months proving it was not me. This was back when everything was done by snail mail, so I had to send in a sheet with my signature written ten times to match the signature on my license. The problem was that I did not even have a license yet, so I had to get my license first before I could resolve the tax issue.

After that ordeal, I finally received my tax refund and bought my first car—a lime-green Volkswagen Beetle. It meant everything to me, especially because I bought it myself, and it was in my favorite color. With my new car, I moved on to other things, focusing on school, work, and hanging out when I could. I began spending less time with the Moore family, creating distance between us. There was no bad blood; I was just outgrowing that lifestyle, and it became noticeable. I reached a point where I felt in control of my own destiny. I no longer needed to do things just to fit in or be accepted. Until then, I felt like my life's path had been hijacked, and I was always just doing what I had to at the moment. Once I turned eighteen and could make my own decisions, I chose to do only what felt right and beneficial for me.

Even though I had started making positive changes in my life, I was still only eighteen, and partying was always on the agenda. One Cinco de Mayo, Shannon, I, and a few friends ended up at a hotel party. I think we crashed it because I cannot even remember who we were there for. As we were leaving, we walked through the hotel kitchen and came across the liquor fridge full of bottles.

Naturally, we grabbed some and started drinking straight from the bottle.

When it was time to go home, Shannon and I raced across the 110 freeway. If you are familiar with the drive from Pasadena to L.A., you know the 110 near Dodger Stadium is full of winding roads. I was in the lead, when I drove through a puddle, the car hydroplaned spinning me out of control. It felt like I was in a bumper car. My car hit the center divider, spun in a complete circle, slammed into the outside wall, and then spun again before crashing back into the center divider. I was so drunk that I got out and threw my shoe at the car as if it were to blame.

Shannon was far behind me and did not see the accident, so by the time she caught up, I was already out of the car. We moved it to the side of the road, and I got into her car to go home. I was so shaken that I could barely sit still. Shannon handed me my first cigarette and said, "Smoke this; it'll calm you down." To my surprise, it worked.

The next morning, Shannon and I woke up, getting ready for the day, singing and dancing like nothing had happened. When I went outside and did not see my car, I screamed, thinking it had been stolen.

Shannon looked at me and said, "Girl, you wrecked your car last night." Suddenly, everything came flooding back, and I could not believe it. I went into a panic again, and the only thing that calmed me down was another cigarette.

Wrecking my car humbled me fast and brought me back to reality. I found myself calling my dad again because I needed his help. He was never the "I told you so" type or someone who made me feel worse when I messed up. Instead, he would step in and clean up the mess when he could. My dad understood that growing up meant I was going to make some inevitable mistakes like drinking, smoking, or hanging out with the wrong crowd. He tried to be the cool dad by letting me and my friends drink at the house, hoping it would keep us from being out on the roads and making bad decisions.

While my car was getting fixed, I struggled in school, so I finally decided to take some time off to get myself together. I was still working at both Bank of America and Banana Republic, but eventually, I felt like BofA was a fraud. Do not judge me for what I am about to say. Remember, I was young and inexperienced. At BofA, we got paid every

Friday, and over the weekend, I would swipe my card everywhere, keeping an eye on my balance as I went. But come Monday morning, I was always in the negative, and by Friday, my whole paycheck would be gone to cover it.

I did not fully understand how swiping debit versus credit worked then. The part that felt like a fraud to me was getting hit with a $25 insufficient funds fee for something like a $1 bag of chips. It felt like I was working just to pay fees. Needless to say, BofA was no longer a good fit for me, and I cut ties with them both professionally and personally.

One day, I was in Pasadena just hanging out and decided to walk to the corner store since the weather was nice. As I was walking, a man suddenly jumped off a porch and stepped out of the yard, blocking me from continuing down the sidewalk. In an aggressive tone, he demanded, "Where is your momma? I have not seen that bitch in a minute, and she owes me money."

I was completely shocked, not even realizing at first that he was talking about my mother. His tone had me so shaken I could not find the words to respond. Before I could say anything, he added,

"You tell Janet if I do not get my money before the next time I see you, I will let you repay her debt. I like what I see." Then he licked his lips in the most disgusting way before walking back into the yard.

That was my final straw, and I was ready to disappear and leave everything and everyone behind. I no longer wanted to be known as Janet's daughter, Michelle, and Amber's little sister, or the girl who was always fighting. I wanted a fresh start, a chance to reinvent myself. Once my car was out of the shop, I packed it up, transferred my Banana Republic job to the Caesars Palace location on the Strip, and moved to Las Vegas.

Chapter XVI

Viva Las Vegas

Welcome me to Vegas, baby! I was eighteen, free to be myself, and back in my dad's good graces. When I was younger, one of my many dreams was to move away, get married, and start my own family. I always envisioned myself becoming the family matriarch, hosting all the holiday and Sunday dinners without the "big mama" part. For now, Las Vegas, Nevada, was just my first stop on that journey.

When I moved to Las Vegas, I was overjoyed. I would finally be closer to my sisters and five nieces and nephews. It had been years since I had been with my biological family. Michelle left when I was thirteen and Amber when I was fourteen, so I had not seen them in about 4-5 years. It felt like getting to know strangers, honestly. We were not close even when we lived in the same house because of our age differences and clashing personalities. With them moving away, we had all grown into completely different people.

Leaving California was my first step toward reinventing myself. I was determined to leave the fighting and street life behind and become a better, greater version of myself. Moving to Vegas marked my fresh start. I had no idea what life in Vegas would be like. I had only been there once for a one-day drill team tournament. I did not know where my sisters worked or how they lived, but I assumed life had to be better than what we had back home in California, especially since they never returned.

Just as I was moving to Vegas, my mother was leaving. When I said she was on an extended drug binge, I was not exaggerating. For two years, my mother claimed she still had her job, and to be honest, we all thought she was lying. She had already been out of work for a year in California before moving to Vegas, where she stayed for another year. Then, a week before I moved to Vegas, she decided she was done with drugs and ready to return to work. Just like that, she was back at her same job and living in a two-bedroom apartment in Inglewood. Apparently, she had been on a leave of absence the whole time, continuously extending it. I have said it before and will always believe it. When my mother wants to do something, she will make it happen. If she does not, it is not because she cannot, but because she did not want to. Without any rehab, she jumped right back into being the mother she was before her relapse.

Although her recovery should have filled me with gratitude, it was bittersweet. I could not help but wonder. If she could turn her addiction on and off, why did she let things get so bad? I went through so much after she relapsed. From 14 to 18, I felt alone, displaced, mentally lost, hurt, and heartbroken. Those were critical years of my life marked by betrayal. I never expressed these feelings to my mother or dwelled on them. Instead, I accepted the situation as a win because, in the end, my ultimate prayer was for her to be sober.

When my mother lived in Vegas, she had a two-bedroom apartment for herself and Jaxon. Right before she left, Amber moved in and took over the apartment in my mother's name. Before I arrived,

Amber offered me a place to stay with her, her two children, and their dad. It was only meant to be temporary until I got settled in the new town. Shortly after I arrived, my car started having issues, so it was back in the shop. I worked at Banana Republic and quickly picked up a second job at a furniture store, with both jobs on opposite sides of town. My days were long. I woke up, took the bus to Banana Republic for a 5-hour shift, then took another bus for an hour to work another 5-hour shift at the furniture store. After that, I had a two-hour bus ride home. I was never home.

Amber is a bit OCD when it comes to cleaning. She cleans before going to bed, wakes up, and cleans. With two small children, I understood. She would wake up and start vacuuming around me on my days off while I slept on the living room floor. Yes, I was sleeping on the floor because she and her baby daddy had one bedroom, and the kids had the other. She did not want me to be on her couch, but I did not mind since she let me stay there. By my third week, it was time for rent, and to my surprise, she asked for half. I was caught off guard but did not want to cause any issues, so I paid up. The next week, she told me the light bill was due, and when

I asked how much, it turned out to be hundreds of dollars—months overdue. Not wanting to rock the boat, I helped pay that, too, feeling like I had no choice.

By the fourth week, things started to feel overwhelming. Even though I was just sleeping on the floor, the cost of staying there was high. Amber was constantly cleaning around me, huffing and puffing as if I were in the way, and the arguments between her and her baby daddy made things uncomfortable. One day, I went to 7/11 and noticed an apartment nearby advertising a $99 move-in special with the first month free. I thought, "I've got $100; let's see what this is about." After about an hour of showing my pay stubs and bank information, they handed me the keys to my new apartment. I could not believe it. When I saw the lights were already on in the unit, I rushed back to Amber's place and excitedly told her I had just gotten my own spot. I immediately started packing. I figured if I was going to sleep on the floor, it might as well be my own.

After I told Amber about the apartment, I called my dad to share the good news. He was so proud of me. Within a few days, he showed up with a U-Haul full of furniture. Since LA was only a 50-minute flight away, he started flying in once a week to have lunch with me and grocery shopping.

I flipped the switch one day, and the lights did not work. Confused, I told my dad something was wrong with the lights. His first question was if I had transferred the utilities into my name. I was completely lost and said, "They were already on when I moved in." He laughed—probably until he was blue in the face. In true Samuel fashion, he took care of everything and even set me up on autopay using his bank card.

Now that I was settling, I decided to try school again. I still did not qualify for financial aid, but my dad offered to pay. I quit my jobs and applied for classes, but never actually started. My plans took a different turn while waiting for the semester to begin. My dad started giving me a weekly allowance of $2,500 because his hustle was thriving then. With that kind of money, I partied nonstop, like it was 1999 all over again. It was the peak of the Hyphy movement, and although I was still underage, when you are buying bottles and tables in Vegas, no one asks for ID.

Chapter XVII

Socializing

Las Vegas was a nonstop party, and I started making new friends both in and outside of the clubs. Amber was more into the nightlife than Michelle, who usually worked and only came out occasionally. Amber introduced me to one of her coworker's turned friend, Jala. She was down for anything and always up for a good time. She also introduced me to another friend, Cheyenne, who was older than all of us but could out-party everyone. Cheyenne was a blast to be around. She always wants to laugh, eat, and just enjoy life.

We were regulars at this club called 702, and it was the most fun ratchet spot I have ever been to. It was so hood they had metal detectors at the entrance. We went so often that we became popular regulars. As Cali girls, we stood out, looked different, moved differently, and outshined every other woman in the place. Our entire week revolved around finding the perfect outfits for both Friday and Saturday nights. Yes, it was that serious!

Naturally, we would mix and mingle, but dancing was my thing back then. I loved it and would be on the dance floor from when we arrived until we left. There was this group of guys who were regulars, too. They are a mix of guys from Louisiana, the Bay Area, and a Las Vegas native. Amber was into one of them, while I enjoyed the company of his friend, Jason, who was from New Orleans. Jason was the dancer of their crew, and we often found ourselves lost in the music on the dance floor, moving like no one else was around. Our chemistry was undeniable; whether he led, or I did, we were always in sync, like we had rehearsed for years.

Things between Jason and me started moving beyond the club scene, and we eventually began leaving together after nights out. We did not talk much during the week; it was more of a weekend thing, a guaranteed link-up after the club. The first time Jason came over without it being just a nightcap, he brought the smallest, cutest little baby

I had ever seen. When I asked whose baby, it was, he told me it was his son. His mother had dropped the baby off when he was only three days old; by this time, he was just two weeks old. I felt immediate sympathy for Jason, but I admired him when he said, "It is fine. I have my little man, and he will always have me." That melted my heart. Jason was twenty-two, working for a window installation company, had a car, and was living with family, so it seemed like he had things under control for the time being.

I kept seeing Jason casually, but I did not want to get too involved since he had a baby, and I was still only eighteen, sneaking into clubs bumping and jumping.

Things slowed down a bit when everyone started working at this popular call center. It seemed like everyone in Vegas worked there at some point. The place was called Sitel, and they were always hiring, giving anyone a job. It felt more like a day party than work, and after shifts, everyone would head to Cheyenne's place to unwind. I was not working then; my dad was still giving me an allowance and covering my bills, so I would be home all day, just waiting for everyone to get off work. Eventually, I wanted to be part of the "club Sitel" crowd, too, so I decided to apply. I got hired, and just like that, I worked with Amber, Cheyenne, and a few other people I had met.

Working at Sitel was a blast, maybe too much fun, because it didn't take long before I got let go. I had a bad attitude toward the "team leads" or anyone acting like they had authority over me. My mentality was that I did not need the job, which was true since I was really only working out of boredom. Looking back, it was not the smartest move because I ended up back to being bored at home while waiting for everyone to get off work. But since Las Vegas is full of call centers, I just got another job. I cannot remember the place's name, but it was shady. We were a third-party collection agency, basically harassing people and breaking all kinds of regulations.

While working at that shady collection agency, I met Adam, who was as cool as they came. We hit it off right away as friends. Adam was a ladies' man, but we were alike in so many ways. I have always had a thing for fashion, and even when I could not afford the best clothes, I still made everything look good, and my confidence just elevated. Adam was the same: well-groomed, cocky, and sure of himself. He had this "for sure" attitude, meaning he was confident in his beliefs and did not care what anyone else thought. We sat next to each other at work, spending our entire shifts laughing and talking. Adam came from a well-off family; his brother was famous, and his mother was rich. But Adam was rebellious, carving his own path and refusing to rely on handouts. Despite his choices, he stayed close to his family, who always ensured he was okay, even though he worked and maintained his own life.

The move to Las Vegas was not too difficult for me. I did not really get homesick since it was only a three-and-a-half-hour drive away. During my first year, I went back home at least twice a month to see my dad and catch up with everyone else. After one of those trips, I was at work scrolling through my digital camera when Adam spotted a picture of Shannon. His eyes lit up, and he flashed a huge smile, barely able to say, "Who is that?" I told him she was my favorite cousin who lived in LA. Right away, he asked me to call her so he could ask for her number, and I did just that.

I called Shannon, and she and Adam exchanged numbers, immediately hitting it off. I think she may have mentioned him once before I asked Adam how things were going. His response shocked me: "She's moving in with me next week." I was amazed, considering they had only met over the phone two weeks prior, and now their first in-person meeting would be her moving across state lines. I was not too worried since Adam seemed like a good guy from what I knew, but Shannon had not asked me much about him before making such a big decision. She confirmed it when I spoke to her, and I was genuinely excited. The next week, Shannon became a Nevada resident.

Since Shannon and Adam were in their honeymoon phase, I did not see much of her at first. We talked occasionally, but she had transferred her job from LA, so her days were spent working, and her evenings were devoted to her new love. Meanwhile, I had already quit my shady job and was back to partying like a rock star. Our new hangout was a spot called Poetry, located inside Caesar's Palace on the Strip. This was a more upscale club where we partied alongside pro athletes and rappers. Poetry was our weekend hotspot, but we were out every night from Monday to Sunday. We explored a different casino or club each night, most closed around 6 AM. Often, when we left Drai's, the sun would already be up.

Chapter XVIII

Sisters

Shortly after I moved into my apartment, Michelle moved into the same complex but in a different building on the opposite end of the complex. Her place was practically empty, and she had almost nothing. Unlike Amber and me, who preferred a fully furnished home, Michelle had no decor whatsoever. Although she maintained a job, she never purchased anything for her apartment. Whenever my dad visited me, he would naturally check in on her. After seeing her apartment, he offered to help, as was typical of him.

I cannot remember how he helped her, but his priority was getting the kids some bunk beds. He was still flying in regularly to take me to lunch and grocery shopping, but then he started buying enough food for Michelle and her kids as well. When I noticed him adding extra items and kid supplies to the cart, I asked him what he was doing.

He explained that he wanted to ensure I had everything I needed at my place because he was concerned about how she was living. Michelle was hardly ever home, leaving the kids alone. My dad had a big heart but did not want to overstep his boundaries. Michelle expected a lot from others, as if she were owed something. He did not want to get caught up in those expectations but wanted to ensure they had food available.

During one of my dad's visits, we were all sitting around chatting when Michelle mentioned she saw a car for sale that she was interested in, but she did not have the money and would have to wait until her next paycheck. My dad told her it might not be available by then and urged her to act quickly, giving her the money to purchase the car. He wanted to ensure she and the kids had reliable transportation for the upcoming winter, especially since she disliked taking the bus when I was not available to give her a ride.

Michelle did end up buying the car, an older Mercedes with high mileage and mechanical issues. It turned out to be a lemon. She had it for only two weeks before it completely broke down. She and the kids were over one night, and it got late. Michelle asked if she could borrow my car to drive them home because it was too cold for the kids to walk. I was hesitant since I had just gotten my car back three days earlier. My dad had it painted burgundy, with peanut butter-colored seats, and my name stitched in the same burgundy as the exterior. It was too cold for me to take them myself, so I agreed, figuring she only had to drive around the complex to her building.

The next morning, Michelle and the kids returned, and I made a big breakfast for everyone. We ate, talked, laughed, and even watched a movie. At some point, Michelle casually said, "Oh yeah, I hit your car last night pulling out of your parking spot." I figured she must have hit the pole next to where I park, so I jumped up, hoping she was joking. But when I went outside, I saw she had scraped the car from the front to the back, completely damaging the entire passenger door. I was furious. I could not believe that instead of telling me right away, she had gone home, then returned, hung out for hours, and only casually mentioned the damage.

Ironically, Michelle did not think it was a big deal and felt my reaction was over the top because I was crying and asking her why she would still go home. Instead of being apologetic, she caught an attitude and started arguing with me. As she walked away, she yelled, "Just call your dad!" as if that was the solution. There was no discussion about how she planned to fix the damage because she clearly had no intention of doing so. I was appalled. Who does something like that and feels no responsibility? This incident and Amber trying to nickel and dime me for a spot on her living room floor made me realize I did not truly know my sisters. They were different in ways I had not expected.

I called my dad and told him someone had randomly hit my car in the apartment parking lot. Technically, it was not a lie; I just did not mention that the "random" person was Michelle, especially since he had just bought her a car. As usual, he flew in to take care of the repairs, and the entire door had to be replaced. That car had been through so much; this was the third time it needed bodywork. I do not think any of the original exterior was left at this point, considering how many times it had been wrecked and swapped out. The outside looked good, and that is all I seemed to care about, which led to more questionable decisions on my part.

I never kept up with the maintenance on the car; no oil changes, no fluid checks, nothing I was supposed to do. I would just fill it up with gas and drive up and down the 215 freeway between Vegas and LA. In my mind, since the car looked good, it must be fine. But I quickly learned that bodywork and proper maintenance are two entirely different things. One day, Amber asked me to borrow my car to go to the store right across the street. After she came out, the car would not start. She called me, and I walked over to meet her. It was not anything she had done; the car was simply on its last leg.

When I arrived, I could do nothing, so I tore a page from the phone book hanging by the pay phone and called a tow company. The tow driver handed me paperwork with details about where the car was being taken, which I stuffed in my back pocket. Amber and I walked back across the street to my apartment, and as soon as we got in, I noticed Mother Nature had started, so I tossed my clothes in the washer and jumped in the shower. Mid-shower, I realized the papers were still in my pants pocket. They were completely ruined when I pulled them out of the washing machine. I did not panic immediately, thinking they would call me for more information or payment at some point.

After a few days with no word, I returned to the payphone, where I grabbed the page from the phone book and found that the book was gone. I had no idea which company I had called, and looking through another phone book did not jog any memories. I was at a complete loss. In the meantime, my dad started renting cars for me, hoping someone would eventually contact me. Every week, I was driving a different high-end rental. Since I was cruising around Vegas in fast, foreign cars, I eventually stopped searching for my car and just accepted that I had somehow lost it, like literally misplaced a whole car.

As my 19th birthday approached, the only gift I had in mind was a new car since I did not have one. I had planned to spend my birthday in California with friends, hoping to be close to my dad in case he decided to get me a car, so I would be there to receive it. A few days before my birthday, we went to our usual breakfast spot, and afterwards, he unexpectedly got on the freeway. When I asked where we were headed, he simply said, "You'll see." When I saw his blink signal exiting near the Felix car dealership, I nearly gasped; I knew exactly where we were going. The huge Felix sign was visible from the exit, confirming my suspicion.

As we pulled up, there was a row of brand-new 2006 Chrysler 300s in assorted colors, each with a bow on top. When I exited the car, my dad said, "Happy Birthday, baby. Pick a color." But instead of being excited, I burst into tears and shouted that I wanted an Audi, my dream car. The sales associate quickly stepped in, giving me a stern look as if he were my own father. He said, "You are being so ungrateful. This man spent hours here filling out paperwork and bragging about you. Your dad is so proud of you and loves you deeply. I have never seen a father come in and buy his daughter a brand-new car with only six miles on it; you should be on your knees thanking him.

I quickly pulled myself together and picked a color. I knew I had been out of line, but I had my heart set on an Audi. Still, I thanked my dad and was truly grateful. Once I got behind the wheel, I realized how much I loved the car. I drove it back to Vegas, feeling on top of the world. Suddenly, I was driving to the valet parking lot and buying sections at all the hot spots. I was convinced nineteen was going to be my year. I didn't have any specific plans for my life then; I was just enjoying the fact that things were finally looking up for me.

Amber and I were still hanging out with Cheyenne and Jala, but one night, just the two of us went to Poetry Night Club. We did not get a section that night, but it was not long before we were invited into the section of three artists who were currently topping the charts. We partied with them all night, and their section had a balcony view overlooking the casino. As Amber glanced down, she spotted one of the guys she was dealing with walking with a group of girls, heading toward the exit. I noticed her making a phone call while leaving the section. One of the artists noticed her in the casino and asked where she was going. With the loud music, I assumed she had stepped down to make her call.

Maybe ten minutes later, the party wrapped up shortly after, but Amber never returned. I went to the casino area to look for her, realizing she had my phone and car keys since I did not carry a purse. When I got to the parking lot, my car was gone. I ran into one of the bouncers I knew and asked if I could borrow his phone to call my sister. Amber's phone was disconnected, so I called mine. When she picked up, I asked, "Where are you, and why did you leave with my car?" She told me she had seen her guy friend leaving with someone and that she was following him. I told her not to chase him and to bring me my car, but she started yelling and cursing so loudly that even the bouncer could hear her. She shouted, "I will bring you your damn car, it is not that serious. I am not doing anything to your car!" The problem was that I had just gotten the car a couple of months ago, Amber did not have a license, and we were on the Las Vegas Strip.

The bouncer, being a gentleman, stayed with me until Amber returned. She came speeding into the parking lot with the headlights off, and I could not believe what I saw. When she got out of the car, still yelling as if I had taken her car and left her stranded, I started yelling back, telling her she had not even turned on the headlights. As I drove off, making a left turn through a four-way intersection, Amber suddenly put my car in park while I was still driving. The car made all kinds of noises. She then flung open the door, grabbed my 22-inch weave ponytail, and tried to drag me out of the driver's seat through the passenger door because I had said she took my car to chase after a guy, which is exactly what she did.

Of course, she could not drag me over the middle console, so I yanked my hair free, got out of the car, walked around to her side, and ended up beating Amber until she was bloody. It was our first fight, and she pushed me in the worst way. I went at her like she was a random threat on the street. We had been having a great night, and I had not done anything to deserve it. She was not angry with me; she was upset with the guy and took it out on me because she could not catch him. The bouncer was in his car right behind me and stepped in to break us up. I got back in my car and left her there.

I remember it like it was yesterday: pulling up to my apartment and putting the key in the door. Just as I turned the key, my phone rang. It was an unknown number, but it was 4 a.m., so I answered. On the other end was Amber, crying and apologizing, saying it was dark back there and she did not have a phone or a way home, begging me to come back and get her. I gave in and went to pick her up. But as I pulled up, I saw police cars everywhere. I tried to drive through, but an officer stepped in front of my car, signaling for me to stop. He said, "Kori White, please get out of the car." I was in shock, asking what was going on, explaining I had come to pick up my sister. The officer replied, "Yeah, she used my phone. You are under arrest for assault and battery with a weapon." Amber told the police I beat her using a high-heeled shoe, which was a total lie.

By this time, Amber had finally reached the guy she had been chasing, and she asked him to get her. He showed up with a friend of his who had a crush on me, and that friend asked the police if he could drive my car home to avoid it being towed. With my permission, he took my car and parked it while I went to jail. Later, he told me that he tried to bail me out and asked Amber for my last name, but she refused to tell him. Since it was 5 a.m. on a Saturday, I was jailed until Monday morning.

I kept trying to call my dad, but he declined my calls. When he finally answered, he did not let me say a word. Apparently, Amber had called him first and told him I was in jail for a DUI. He gave me an earful, telling me that he had already flown into town, taken my car back to California, and that I was too irresponsible to have it. I never got the chance to tell him she had lied or explained what really happened. He did not accept any more of my calls after that. My dad had never treated me that way before; he was a different type of mad that I had never seen from him.

Chapter XIX

Life after lockup

Aday and a half is too long to be locked up in jail. I was devastated, not just because my dad did not listen to me but also because Amber had set me up. I have to admit it, she knew she was wrong and started everything but using the police phone to lure me back so I would end up in jail was just cruel. Fortunately, I did not have to go to court, as all the charges were dropped, thanks to my knight in shining armor, the bouncer. He came down to the jail and made a statement on my behalf, explaining everything from the initial phone call to what he witnessed while driving out of the parking lot behind us.

He was not there when I was released, and I never saw him again after that night. Since Shannon was at work, I called Adam to come pick me up. When we arrived at my apartment, just as my dad had said, my car wasn't there; he really did come and repossess it. When I opened the door, I found it had already been unlocked. My niece and nephew were in the living room, with the AC blasting and every light on, watching TV with their dog, while Amber and their dad were in my bed asleep. I was furious; she had no right to be there, had never asked for my permission, and was not even staying there before I was arrested. How dare she make herself at home in my apartment after sending me to jail and lying to my dad? I was completely baffled. I am unsure how long she thought I would be gone, but she even went grocery shopping. I tossed everything over the patio: all the food, her clothes, and even the dog had to go. She had told the kids' dad the same lie she told my dad, but I quickly cleared that up, which exposed her cheating. She left me to chase a guy she saw with someone else and got mad when I called her back before she could catch up to him. The police showed up and told me that I would be going right back to jail if I did not clean up all the stuff Amber did not pick up that I had thrown. It was the fastest turnaround because I could not return to jail.

From that point, things began to fall apart quickly. My apartment lease ended, I was out of a job and had no car and no money, and my dad had completely cut me off. Michelle and I were not speaking because of the previous car situation, and Amber and I were also on bad terms, leaving me with no one to turn to except Shannon and Adam. They lived in a two-bedroom townhouse and offered me a room until I could get back on my feet. I sank into a depression, spending most days in bed while they were at work. One day, while Shannon was out, Adam came into the room and sat at the foot of the bed as I lay under the covers. He started talking and reminding me of the person he first met. His words were filled with positivity, affirmation, and even prayer. I did not say a word, but before leaving, he mentioned that his mom was looking for an assistant and that he would talk to her about me. The next morning, he came in, opened the blinds, and told me to get dressed because his mother would be there that afternoon, and I should consider it an interview. I had no choice but to pull myself together. His mother was a highly successful businesswoman, and only by chance was she visiting her son and agreeing to meet with me.

Despite how intimidating his mother was, she agreed to give me a trial run, and I started immediately. My first task was arranging flights, hotels, and transportation for an upcoming event she and her other son attended in New York. I handled it smoothly, and soon, I was managing task after task, from emails to phone calls and various errands. His mother and I often met for lunch to go over her schedule and discuss assignments she needed me to handle. Initially, she was tough and direct, but she softened over time. She eventually opened up about her late daughter, who had passed away from a rare disease just a year earlier. Although she was still grieving, I could sense that my presence brought her some comfort. She even offered me beauty tips and advice on how a businesswoman should present herself. She once gifted me with a pair of diamond studs, noting that hoops are not suitable for every occasion. We really started to grow on each other.

Not long after I began working for Adam's mother, I could afford my own place again: a one-bedroom apartment on the other side of town. When I shared the news with Shannon, she broke down in tears, admitting she had not been entirely honest with me. She and Adam were not getting along, and things were not as they seemed. She asked if I could change the lease to a two-bedroom so we could live together. Without hesitation, I called the leasing office and arranged for a two-bedroom, two-bath apartment. I did not need their relationship's full details; knowing she was uncomfortable was reason enough. When Shannon's father heard about us moving in together, word quickly returned to my dad. At that point, he had been holding my car for about two months. He finally decided to call me, and once he learned the full story, he was deeply apologetic. He was more disappointed in himself for not giving me a chance to explain, taking Amber's word without hearing my side. He had my car back to me before moving into my new apartment.

Living with Shannon was great. She was still dating Adam, so sometimes, she stayed at his place. They were constantly arguing, mostly about a loan she had taken out for him that he had not repaid, so their relationship was up and down. I had started working at a call center, and soon, Shannon joined me there. Working together was convenient—we took turns driving. Besides working and living together, we also started going out to parties. Shannon had not been part of our Las Vegas party crew before, so it was all new to her. One night, as a pre-birthday celebration, Shannon and I went to Poetry during the week. We met some guys there who celebrated because they had won a case and avoided jail time with house arrest. It was the last night out for one of them before his house arrest began.

After that night at the club, Shannon and the guy spent a lot of time talking on the phone. I would catch bits and pieces of their conversations in passing but never really listened closely. Most of the time, I could hear her complaining about Adam to him, and I would wonder why he would even care. At some point, it felt like she was trying to prove to the guy on the phone that she was not as involved with Adam as she was.

One afternoon, during my lunch break, I received a call from Adam's mother. In a very calm voice, she said, "He is gone. Somebody killed Adam."

Shocked and overwhelmed with disbelief, I started crying hysterically. Everyone around me stopped to help as I felt my knees weaken and my whole-body tremble. Adam's mother asked the person who took my phone to give me a moment to pull myself together, but she really needed to speak with me. When I got back on the phone, she asked where Shannon was, as she could not reach her. I told her that Shannon had returned home, out of town, and that I would call her.

When I called Shannon, she answered right away. Hearing me already in tears, she asked what was wrong, and I told her that someone had killed Adam. She said something quickly and hung up. I assumed she was calling his mother back, having missed all her earlier calls. I composed myself and waited to hear back from Shannon, giving her a moment to process everything. Before I could speak to Shannon again, Adam's mother called me back to share what allegedly happened. It had not even crossed my mind that she would say this occurred at his townhome. He had been murdered in his own home, with no signs of forced entry, and the door had been locked from the outside. She explained that she had tried calling him the night before but got no answer, and when he did not respond the next morning either, she went over and used her key, only to find him in his living room, gone.

I expected Shannon to come back right away, but she stayed in California for a few days after the news before returning, only because detectives requested to speak with her. She seemed so cold about the situation, as if it had not really happened. When she finally came home, her vibe was off, so I gave her space, understanding that everyone grieves in their own way. I thought she would talk about Adam in the days leading up to his service, but she never mentioned him. It was like she had moved on, focusing instead on her new connection with the guy from the club.

Adam's mother reached out to let me know they were holding a private memorial for him out of state. Before we ended the call, she asked about Shannon and Adam's relationship, but I did not have much to offer since they were usually quite private. I had overheard some phone arguments, but nothing out of the ordinary, so I did not feel it was worth mentioning. I knew she was looking for anything that might help his case, but I did not want to add to her pain. She then mentioned she had not heard from Shannon since everything happened, which surprised me. Why wouldn't Shannon check in with her boyfriend's mother after such a tragedy? With a hint of sarcasm, his mother remarked, "I thought she'd have questions about the case or even the services, but I guess not."

Feeling uneasy after that conversation and noticing Shannon's strange behavior around the apartment, I could not help but start thinking. I asked Shannon a few questions, not implying anything. I was simply curious, but she did not like it and quickly became defensive, so I backed off. Over the next few months, Adam's mother continued to call, each time pressing harder for information. I kept telling her I did not know anything. Apparently, there were inconsistencies in the case, and his mother felt that if I knew anything, it could shift the investigation. By this point, I realized she suspected Shannon might be involved in his murder and believed that anything I shared could prompt detectives to look deeper into her.

Shannon and I continued living together for a few months after everything happened, but our connection was not the same. Shannon began to change, influenced largely by her new boyfriend, the guy from the club. She adopted a tough persona that felt completely unlike her. It was like watching my favorite cousin transform into someone unrecognizable. Eventually, she and the guy got an apartment together, and our relationship faded. I would still see her occasionally, but nothing like before. One day, while visiting their place, I mentioned Adam's name, and Shannon gave me a look, almost in fear, shaking her head as if to say not to bring him up. That really left a sour taste in my mouth. How could she avoid talking about someone she claimed to love, someone she lived with and was in a relationship with? Later, she told me it was not that she did not want to; it was because her boyfriend did not want her to. I found it incredibly disrespectful, pushing me to distance myself even more.

Chapter XX

My Co-pilot

Eventually, Amber and I started talking again after she set me up. I cannot quite recall how it happened, but soon, the old crew came back together. Well, almost—Cheyenne was now pregnant. Her focus was food, so we would either have a cookout at her place or go out to eat. One night, a group of us decided to check out a new club inside one of the casinos. When we arrived, six months pregnant, Cheyenne was not feeling up to it, so she stayed in the casino while the rest of us went into the club. I had not been inside long before realizing it was all afrobeats, which was not my scene.

When I found Cheyenne in the casino, she was completely focused on a slot machine. She was between two other people, so I took the nearest seat beside the guy on her left. With him between us, we just kept talking across him as if he wasn't even there. I have always been terrible at gambling, so I rarely do it, but with $20 in my pocket and time to kill, I decided to give it a shot. In just a few spins, all my money was gone. Looking past the guy, I told Cheyenne, "See, this is why I don't gamble; it is because I never win." The guy between us stood up and said, "I'll be right back," as if we had all come together. We exchanged a look and laughed because it was such an unnecessary comment.

When the guy returned, he stood at about 5 foot 2 inches and looked me straight in the eyes as I remained seated. He asked, "Can I teach you how to gamble?" Apparently, when he left and felt the need to announce it, he had gone to the ATM. I stood up, towering over him, and said, "Sure." He extended his hand and said hi, I am Morris Fields, and you are?" I said just Kori, laughed, and we began to walk around the casino. As we passed the machines, he would run his hands along their sides. After passing a few, he stopped at one, inserted a $20 bill, and told me to hit max bet. When I did, we hit the jackpot, winning hundreds of dollars. He pulled out the ticket and handed it to me; then, we moved on to the next machine. He started with five

$20 bills, putting $20 into each machine and telling me to hit max bet again. He also handed me those tickets each time we hit the jackpot or won a considerable sum.

Once all the cash was gone, I tried to hand him the stack of tickets totaling well over a thousand dollars, but he said, "No, that's yours—you won that; you hit max bet." He then asked if he could take me to get steak and eggs from iHop, which was just a few casinos away. I told him I could not because I was with four other girls, and he replied, "They can come too." Just as he said that everyone was walking out. I shared his offer with them, and everyone agreed to join, with Cheyenne being the most excited. When we arrived at iHop and ordered, just as the food was coming out, Cheyenne received a call from her husband, who was out with Amber's boyfriend, asking them to come home. Since I was driving, I had to take them back. I apologized to Morris, explained that I had to go, and asked for his number, telling him I owe him steak and eggs.

The next day, I called him to keep my word. I wanted to get the steak and eggs I owed him. We talked on the phone for hours, laughing and joking like old friends, even though we had just met. That evening, we met at a bar and had an amazing time, so much so that we spent time together every day for the next three months. What made it special was that we had no expectations; our connection grew naturally. We genuinely enjoyed each other's company without any pressure or intimacy. Nearly every other night, we'd go out until six in the morning, and somehow, Morris would still make it to work by 7 a.m.

Morris lived right across the street from his job, so it was easy for him to return home, shower, and head to work. I am not sure how he managed it, though. I never had the energy to drive home, so I usually stayed at his place while he went to work. When we were out, he had this two-drink rule. He would always ensure we both had two drinks: one to finish and one to sip while waiting for the next round. It was a continuous cycle of drinks with him. He loved to party, and we would often be the last ones to leave. There were many nights we spent in parking garages, too drunk to drive home. One morning, after sleeping in a garage, we returned to his place only to find his motorcycle had been stolen. He was heartbroken, especially because he had customized it with unique details. He blamed himself for not coming home that night to block it like usual.

When we hung out, we were a total mess, and Morris loved the attention he got being with me, especially since he was much shorter. It boosted his ego, and I encouraged every bit of it. We had this routine: I would stand at the bar, and within minutes, a guy would come over to talk to me. Morris would be nearby, and when the guy tried to chat, I would say, "Oh, I'm with him." The guy would laugh or say something wild every time, assuming I was joking. That is when Morris would step up, practically standing on his toes, and gives me the nastiest slurp ever. Watching the look on each guy's face made Morris feel a bit taller every time.

During this time, I spent a lot of time at Morris's apartment, and we even exchanged keys to each other's places. I still had my two-bedroom apartment nearby since Shannon had moved out. With all the time we spent together, we naturally talked about our pasts and how we were raised. I shared some key moments from my life, and he did the same. His life was far less chaotic than mine. He grew up as a military brat in a two-parent household with siblings who got along like regular siblings. My experience was different. I was still working through my relationship with my mom and only just really getting to know my sisters. Even after all these years, my mom still treated me differently than them. We also talked about how I had been told I could not have children and how I did not believe in abortion, especially because my mother had tried so hard to end her pregnancy with me.

Morris was quite a bit older than me and already had a son, knowing he did not want more children. When we met, he had just finished an eight-year term in the Air Force. He was originally stationed in Texas, but his first job opportunity brought him to Las Vegas. During his time in the Air Force, he had been in a long-term relationship, lasting about six or seven years. The move to Vegas had strained that relationship, and they eventually decided to part ways. From how he spoke about her, I could tell their love and friendship were still very much there. I remember one day, while he was at work, a package arrived for him. I called to let him know, and he asked me to open it. Inside was a car GPS with a note that read, "Hopefully, one day, you will find your way back to me." It was the sweetest gesture, and it melted my heart. It had come from his ex-girlfriend.

A short time after meeting Morris, my job went through a mass layoff and I was let go. I was not too stressed since it was Vegas, where you could lose a job today, find another tomorrow, and start the next day. I did not start job-hunting immediately because I had just been paid and had my rent money, or so I thought. I cannot remember exactly what happened, but something came up, and I ended up using some of my rent money, leaving me $50 short. I called my mother and asked if she could help, but she said she would rather give the money to Amber to pay her storage bill. I reminded her that Amber often got storage units and lost them because she either did not pay or decided she did not want the stuff anymore. Covering my rent was a better investment, as I was at risk of losing my entire place. But my mother said no and was sure I would figure it out.

Eventually, I figured things out and managed to pay my rent. I was too embarrassed to ask Morris for help; he was already covering so much whenever we went out, and I didn't want to add money issues to that, especially since he knew both Amber and Michelle were constantly in and out of my apartment, staying over because they had nowhere else to go. I always gave them rides without any gas money or help with utilities, even though they were there more than I was. It was almost like I was hiding out at his place most of the time because my sisters and the kids were always at mine, and nine times out of ten, if I were home somehow, I would end up babysitting.

As rent time approached again, I was still without a job and feeling the pressure, trying to figure out a solution. Amber and Michelle had promised to help since they were practically living there, but they never followed through. They both left a few days before rent was due, leaving me to handle everything alone. Amber claimed she could not contribute because the storage unit my mother had paid for the previous month was ruined; they had packed in such a rush after her eviction that they had put open food inside, which caused roach and rat infestation. She said she needed her money to replace her things, while Michelle just went off to a friend's house without saying a word.

One day, knowing my situation, I was at Morris's apartment when he came in from work and handed me a Bank of America envelope. I opened it to find ten crisp $100 bills inside. When I asked him what it was for, he said, "I know your sisters let you down, so use this to pay your rent and have gas money for job hunting and interviews." I was so grateful that I just hugged him, tears running down my face. I agreed to pay him back once I got on my feet, but it was understood that I did not have to.

Morris and I went out on a triple date with four of his friends from his military days, all of whom were his age, about 7-8 years older than me. Over dinner, they discussed everything from politics and careers to travel and current events. I sat there quietly, realizing I had nothing to contribute. I did not have a career, knew nothing about politics, and did not even have a passport. The only "current events" I knew about were which clubs were popular on certain nights and which big-name acts were coming to town. I felt completely out of place at that moment, as if my life were flashing before me. At 20, I had nothing of substance to discuss. That night was a turning point; I stopped reading gossip blogs and started following news articles on Yahoo and CNN. I never wanted to feel so out of touch again, so I made it a point to stay informed and broaden my interests beyond just the party scene.

Soon after, I landed a job at a call center that paid $22 an hour with unlimited overtime. Overjoyed, Morris and I went out to celebrate. That night was unforgettable; everything felt perfect from when I woke up to when we returned to his place. Riding the height of such an incredible day, one thing led to another, and we shared our first intimate moment. We had been hanging out every day for over two months, even sleeping in the same bed, but something about that night took our connection to a whole new level. Because he was older than me, he taught me a few things, and from that moment on, we were like jackrabbits. We could not keep our hands off each other. We would find new and exciting ways to enjoy each other all around Las Vegas; the thrill was the idea of getting caught. Thank goodness we never did, but we came close.

There was a time when one of Morris's friends, a guy he had served with, came into town. This friend had always been the wild card of their group. When he arrived, he asked Morris if he knew any girls who wanted to party. Not knowing exactly what he meant by "party," I invited Amber and Shannon along for the night to show him a good time. It turned out he was looking for a different party type, and Amber and Shannon were unexpectedly on board with it. I was taken aback, thinking, "Wait, what's really going on here?"

That night taught me some disturbing things about Amber and Shannon. I contacted them separately to express my concerns, not realizing just how serious things had become for Shannon. I had already begun distancing myself from her because of how she had handled things after Adam's passing, but this time, I knew I had to cut ties entirely. During my conversation with Shannon, her boyfriend, the guy from the club, made a disturbing threat that closely resembled recent events, leaving me genuinely frightened. When I told Morris, he insisted I stay at his place for the next week, not wanting me to be alone.

For the next few weeks, I immersed myself in my new job, working excessive overtime—12-hour shifts six days a week, with Sundays as my only day off. One afternoon, I grabbed lunch at a Mexican restaurant, and by that evening, my stomach was in turmoil. I tossed and turned all night, moaning in my sleep from the pain. I needed to use the bathroom, but I could not bring myself to do it in Morris's one-bedroom apartment, where the bathroom was in the bedroom. Finally, Morris told me I was disturbing his sleep and that I should just do it if I needed to go. He reassured me it was natural and that he would not judge me.

I took his advice for some reason, but the moment I went in, it was as if a floodgate had opened. I found myself in and out of the bathroom every seven minutes all night, using it repeatedly as if I had never gone before. I was mortified and wanted nothing more than to go home, but with the distance, I knew I would not make it without an accident. So, I had to stay. Morris looked at me the next morning and said, "I didn't even know a human body could produce so much waste." I felt so embarrassed because that was the very judgment he promised he would not have. I had never experienced anything like that before.

Needing a break from the previous night's chaos, I went home to take a nap since I had not slept at all. Both Michelle and I were curled up in my bed when I suddenly woke up craving a glass of water. As I got up, Michelle opened her eyes, and as she looked at me, she said my body just went limp, and I fainted. When I came to, Michelle was standing over me, panicking and asking if I was okay. I told her I had been using the bathroom a lot and was probably just dehydrated. After I laid back down, I was soon jolted awake by loud voices indicating my cousins had stopped by.

I got up to chat with them, and while we were sitting in the living room, Michelle looked at me and said, "Your face is so pale; you look pregnant." Knowing what the doctors had told me, I always kept a pregnancy test under the sink because I had irregular cycles and wanted to check occasionally to ease my mind when I missed one. Without saying a word, I returned to the bathroom to take the test. I did not think much of it as I sat there going through the motions. To my shock, the result came back positive. I could not believe it; I just sat there in disbelief. I must have taken too long because Michelle came looking for me after what had happened earlier. When she opened the bathroom door, the positive test was right there in my hand. I looked up and said man said one thing, and God said another as I turned the test around, showing her the results.

I only had one pregnancy test at home, and I was not sure how old it was, so I went to the store and bought two more. Just like the first, both of those came back positive. Having a baby was not even on my radar; I did not think it was possible. But within minutes of finding out, I felt an overwhelming sense of love. At the same time, I was nervous about what everyone would think. I had always been private in my personal life, and though people might have had suspicions about whether I was sexually active, I'd never confirmed it.

The first person I called was my dad. I was already in tears before he even answered because I did not know how he would react. But when I told him, he was thrilled. He was ready to jump on a flight to meet Morris and start planning the next steps. Then

I called my grandma, struggling to get the words out. I had seen how harsh she had been with Amber and Michelle when they had their first children, expressing her disappointment regularly. But when I told her, she just asked why I was crying. I said I feared her reaction, and she reassured me, saying, "Unlike your sisters, you are grown with a high school diploma, your own place, a job, and the means to care for a child. You have time, but if God chose now, so be it." Talking to her made me feel so much more controlled.

Finally, I called my mom. When I told her, she asked, "How?" I laughed and said, "Do I really need to explain that?" She said, "No, I just thought you were a lesbian." Completely taken aback, I asked why she thought that. She said she assumed it because I had been a tomboy growing up and never seen me with a man. I guess she did not remember the boyfriend I had spent nights with at her place, or maybe she was too out of it to notice.

Later that night, I had plans to meet up with Morris, the one person I was most nervous about telling. We had already had the conversation about my inability to have children and how he did not want anymore. During that talk, I also shared my strong feelings on abortion. We met at a club, and when he went to hand me a drink, I told him I could not have it and explained why. At first, he laughed, thinking I was joking, but he realized I was serious when I did not accept the drink he had already bought.

Chapter XXI

Not who's Dad

Now that the news was out and everyone knew I was pregnant, it was time to start getting things in order. I was thrilled about my first doctor's appointment and went alone, as Morris was still processing everything. He was grappling with the fact that we had both believed I could not have children, yet here I was, clearly pregnant. Given my medical history, I saw it as a blessing and was certain I wanted this baby. Although Morris did not want another child, he never mentioned an abortion; instead, he just accepted the situation as it was.

My first appointment did not go as I had hoped. It was not that I really knew what to expect. They could see the gestational sac during the ultrasound, but there was no heartbeat yet. I was told that the heartbeat typically develops around 6-7 weeks, so it seemed I had discovered my pregnancy quite early. Given my medical history and the absence of a heartbeat, the doctor wanted to be cautious and put me on bed rest for the next two weeks. During that time, I took off work and spent most evenings with Morris.

In the following two weeks, so much unfolded; it was as if time sped up and reality set in. Morris and I had several conversations and agreed that since we had not worked on a relationship before the pregnancy, we did not need to force one now. Our main goal was to prioritize our child and fulfill our roles as parents. Deep down, I knew that Morris was still very much in love with his ex; their split had been due to distance, not a loss of love, and I had come into his life when they thought it was over. Morris also had other concerns I was not aware of then but would come to understand later.

My father's excitement was unmatched. He was thrilled for me and overjoyed at the thought of becoming a grandfather. He did not waste any time coming to Las Vegas to meet the man who had gotten me pregnant. The meeting went well; my dad was impressed with Morris and was ready for us to head to the nearest chapel to get married. Being old-school, he assumed we were in a relationship because I was pregnant and spending time with Morris. I did not know how to tell him that what started as a fling had become a lifelong commitment with no intentions beyond co-parenting.

Morris and I really enjoyed each other's company, whether we were watching a movie or cooking together. We spent a lot of time talking about our lives and upbringings. I shared my hopes for my child, explaining how I wanted to break the generational curses my family had faced and ensure they would not have to experience the things I went through. While I was on bed rest, we did not go out much, but one night, Aunt Dee was in town and wanted to catch up. Being cooped up had gotten boring, so we met her at the New Orleans casino.

As I mentioned before, Aunt Dee was the one who kept us involved in all the church activities and would relate everything back to the gospel. She used to run the streets with my mother but eventually turned her life over to God. While we were sitting at the slot machines, the server offered complimentary drinks. I had never seen Aunt Dee drink before, but she decided to have just one that night at the casino. Of course, neither Morris nor I took one because he was driving and had precious cargo.

I am unsure how the topic came up, but Aunt Dee dropped a bombshell. She talked about a night when she and my mother were out. She reminisced so much that Morris and I started wondering where she was going with this story. At first, I thought she was just tipsy and reliving her wild days. But as she continued rambling, she suddenly said, so casually, "That was the night your mother got raped and became pregnant with you." Now that got my attention, and I asked her to repeat herself, feeling utterly confused. She went on to explain that at a party, a large, dark-complexioned man who played for either the Dallas Cowboys or Houston Texans had forced my mother into a room and taken advantage of her. Then, she added that my father, Samuel, had taken a liking to me from the moment I was born and decided to claim me as his own.

I was speechless, unable to find a single word. I just sat there, staring blankly. Morris asked me, "Why do you look like this is your first time hearing this?" I replied, "Because it is." He immediately stood up and said, "Let's go." We barely managed a quick goodbye to Aunt Dee as we hurried toward the exit. The ride home was eerily silent. Neither of us seemed to know how to process what had just been revealed. A lot was racing through my mind, but I kept it all to myself, knowing I needed to talk to my mother before doing anything else.

I barely slept, tossing, and turning all night as I thought about how to ask my mother if Aunt Dee's claims were true. The next day, I called her and bluntly asked, "Is my dad my real dad?" Confused, she replied, "Why would you ask something like that?" I explained what Aunt Dee had told me, and without hesitation, she confirmed it but immediately added that this was not a topic she wanted to discuss. Naturally, I had questions, but my mother quickly shut me down.

Lost and confused, my heart shattered not just because I discovered my dad was not my biological father but because everything began to make sense.

The signs had always been there; I was too young to see them. Memories played in my mind as if they were paused, waiting for me to sit still and reflect. I grew up being treated very differently from my siblings. I remember asking my mother why she treated me that way when I was only 7 or 8. I never realized I was a constant reminder of her trauma. Her holiday story about trying to abort me and giving me up for adoption was not a moment of grace but one filled with deep regret. When my sisters would say, "That's why Samuel isn't your real dad," she never corrected or punished them for it. And then there was Grandma Louis, who never seemed to care for me and always favored her godchild over me. Everyone knew the truth except for me, and I could not believe how many people knew it.

Whenever I needed my dad for legal matters, he never showed up. He was always there for me, so I never understood why he allowed the courts to take me. Now I realize he had no legal authority over me; he was not my biological father, was not listed on my birth certificate, and was not exactly a law-abiding citizen. While he could not help me in certain situations, he always did what he could.

Learning that he was not my biological father only deepened my love and respect for him in ways I never thought possible. He had always been my dad, but now he felt like my hero.

The way my father loved me blood relation could not bring us any closer. He had countless opportunities to walk away, give up on me, or treat me differently, yet he never did. He never hinted or acted like I was not his child. As I reflected on everything, I wondered if he might have remained unaware of the truth, especially if my mother had lied to him. My dad often bragged about how much I looked and acted like him, as if the split between him and my mother was 70/30, with his genes accounting for the seventy. He was my protector; I could do no wrong in his eyes. He always made it a point to ensure I was happy, and no matter what the situation, my happiness was his main priority.

At this time, I was twenty and pregnant. My emotions and hormones were all over the place, and I was struggling to make sense of a whirlwind of unknown feelings. I was pregnant by a guy I barely knew; I had just discovered that my father was not my biological dad, and I learned I was the product of rape, which explained why my mother could not fully love me as a mother should. The only thing I was certain of was that I would not mention or question my dad about any of this.

When I discovered the truth about my dad, it felt as though our roles had reversed—he had gone from protecting me to me feeling the need to protect him. For the past 20 years, he had made a promise he never wavered from. Once he accepted me as his child, everything changed. How could I question him when he had earned his place in my life? I felt that opening Pandora's Box would only cause him pain. He made a selfless decision and remained committed to me, and I did not want to take that away from him. If he knew that I knew the truth, he would also have to confront the reality of the situation. I did not feel the need to try to fix what society would call broken. The life he had created for me was everything I needed, and my appreciation was to never make him feel like his fatherhood was in question.

One might expect my dad's next call or visit to be awkward, but it was nothing of the sort. It felt as if I had never learned anything at all. The only difference was that when I looked at him, I truly saw him. I saw a man of his word, a man of integrity, a man with a heart of gold. I saw a hand-delivered blessing from God Himself. God knew I needed him, and he needed me. As a product of rape, with my mother struggling with that pain, God provided me with a dad who would love me unconditionally, instill my values, and show me the possibilities of life. I had no control over how my early life turned out, my mother's struggles, or the distance between my siblings and me, but circumstances placed me right in the center. God gave me my dad to protect my heart from everything that was meant to break me emotionally. My dad was always my beacon of hope after every tribulation, the ones I knew about and the ones that were buried.

Chapter XXII

Swept Under the Rug

As I prepared for my new life as a mother, I was still processing my past. Once I decided not to discuss the situation with my father, I did not consider bringing it up again. My mother, however, was another matter; I craved answers. I needed to know what had happened; did she know this man from the neighborhood? Did she report the incident? Why hadn't she told me before? Was this the reason she cared for me instead of loving me? How could we rebuild our relationship without the weight of that trauma? Unfortunately, I never got the chance to ask her anything. Each time I tried, she refused to engage; after my initial inquiry, she hung up on me the next time I asked. I figured I would resolve that by making sure it would be in person the next time I asked so she could not simply end the conversation.

I was taken aback by how many people already knew about my situation. Everyone seemed aware of this secret but ignored it, brushing it aside as if it were nothing worth discussing. I could understand if there had not been any lingering effects, but in this case, the signs of bitterness toward my existence were clear. I could not help but wonder if my older cousins took me for the day or let me spend the night with them as a way to protect my innocence. Did they notice the difference in the way my mother treated me and tried to shelter me whenever they could? One thing that always resonated with me growing up was everyone's conviction that I would be different and achieve remarkable things. It felt like people constantly pulled me aside to offer words of affirmation. They would tell me that I would be my mother's best child, succeed regardless of my challenges and that God had a purpose for me. I always thought they said those things because I was so different from my sisters, but now I realize they might have felt I needed to hear it because they knew I had been dealt an unfair hand from birth.

While getting to know Morris, he came into my life during an incredibly chaotic time. Then again, any time might have felt hectic, but this time, it really was not of my own making. He witnessed things unfolding in real time, taking us both by surprise. Normally, when you are getting to know someone, you share your past, talk about how much you have grown, and reflect on how you have changed for the better. I shared some parts of my childhood with Morris, like my time in foster care, without going into much detail and my delinquent ways. I knew it probably painted a picture of instability in his mind. Still, I told him confidently, knowing I had left that lifestyle behind in California and had genuinely changed.

I had no way of knowing that Morris would end up witnessing a new phase of dysfunction in my life, one I had not even seen coming. I thought I had left chaos behind, but it turned out that I was stepping into a new set of deeper, darker issues that had been quietly brewing for years. I often say I truly met my sisters when I moved to Las Vegas. The young girls I thought I had known from before were now women I barely recognized. I had already been in Vegas for just over a year when I met

Morris. I had noticed signs that my sisters were going through something, but I had written it off as a temporary phase. Unfortunately, who they had become and who I used to be started to paint a picture of who I still was, in Morris's eyes.

Within just the first three months of getting to know Morris, he had already seen more than I ever expected. He learned about my close friend's murder, which had its own cloud of suspicion. Both of my sisters had been evicted and had moved into my place; I lost my job, he paid my rent, I found out I was pregnant, and I discovered the truth about my father. It was a lot for everyone to process. I believe that when things started to really sink in, Morris slowly realized that this was what his life might look like for the next 18 years. I remember we started spending less time together, and I went home more often. We would still talk and hang out, but not nearly as much. I could tell he did not want to get any closer than we already were.

The breaking point between Morris and me came after a situation with Amber and Shannon. I am unsure if Amber stayed with Shannon and the club guy, but I knew they went out every night. I had been watching Amber's kids, but I refused once I found out what they were really up to, hoping it would encourage her to stay home. Instead, Amber, determined to keep going out, left my six-year-old niece with the club guy's grandmother, who lived in a house where drugs were sold. I was furious, calling Amber and telling her she was wrong about leaving her child in an environment like that, with strangers constantly coming and going. When she stopped answering my calls, I decided to reach out to my mother. In the process of telling on Amber's behavior, Shannon's actions came to light as well. Before long, I was on the phone with everyone, explaining why someone needed to step in and do something.

They did not take that well at all. Once again, the club guy arrived with threats, but this time, they were aimed at my unborn child. Amber and Shannon went as far as to reach out to Morris on MySpace, claiming that the baby I was carrying was not his and that I was trying to pin it on him for his money. But Morris did not believe a word of it. From the first day we met, we had been together every day until I found out I was pregnant, so I could not have been with anyone else. And as for the money they thought he had, let me just say it was not nearly enough to make anyone plot like that. But this was the moment that caused Morris to fully detach. From then on, our communication dwindled to text and email only.

After some time had passed, Morris and I started chatting occasionally. I mentioned that I was considering transferring my job to California since there was a site close to a house my godbrother was renting out. He replied with words of encouragement and mentioned he was also exploring a job opportunity in Colorado. But just a few days later, I was let go of my job. The reason given was that my numbers had dropped for the month due to the two weeks I had taken off. I was devastated; they knew why I had been out. Other than that, I was fully committed to the job, working daily, and saving as much as possible, especially with unlimited overtime.

One day, I was at home sleeping on the couch when I woke up with a strange craving. Most pregnant women crave unusual food combinations, but mine was different. It is hard to explain, but I craved the smell of my mother, a scent she did not even have. It was more like a longing for her presence, though it felt like a scent I needed. The craving seemed to grow stronger each day until finally, I called Michelle. I asked if she were still staying with a friend, and when she said yes, I told her she could have my fully furnished two-bedroom apartment because I was going to live with Mom. All I wanted was to sleep in her bed, just like I did when I was younger.

I talked to my dad daily, and he knew I had been let go of my job. He was confused about why I had moved to California and left Morris in Las Vegas, especially since he had high hopes for our relationship. It was hard to tell him the true nature of things. I planned to eventually, but I decided to put it off for now with so much happening. I did not lie to him; I just did not mention that Morris and I barely spoke.

When I arrived in California, my first task was to contact my apartment complex in Las Vegas to inform them of my move. I knew the leasing agents fairly well, so they understood my situation with a high-risk pregnancy and the need to be near family.

I explained that my sister Michelle was interested in taking over the lease. However, when they checked her background, they found she had an outstanding balance at another complex, which prevented her from subleasing. They agreed to let her stay because she had agreed to pay off her balance and reapply for my unit. To help her save money to clear up her debt, I covered the rent in full for the first month, paid half the second month, and planned for her to take over entirely by the third month.

In the third month, I got a call from the leasing office informing me that they had only received partial payment for the previous month and nothing for the current month. Michelle had not paid any rent during the three months she had been there, nor had she cleared her debt to qualify for the apartment. The office, sympathetic to my situation, told me they did not want to add to my stress and offered to terminate my lease without eviction or balance if I could have the apartment cleared by the following weekend. When I called Michelle to explain the situation, she immediately became enraged, accusing me of putting her and her kids out with nowhere to go. I tried to explain that it was not my choice; her failure to pay the rent left no other option.

In the days leading up to the weekend move, I was six months pregnant, waddling around to get things done. My dad, still puzzled about why he had not heard much about Morris, decided to give him a call. During their conversation, Morris was straightforward about our situation and told my dad that we had agreed to co-parent but were not planning to be together. I had not had the chance to tell Morris I had moved back to California, as everything happened so quickly after losing my job. When my dad mentioned I was in California, Morris assumed I had transferred jobs, as I had mentioned previously. My dad, however, told him I was unemployed and staying with my mother. The whole situation made it look like I had been keeping things from both, but the truth was simply that I had not kept them updated, and they were both working with old information.

My dad was furious. He thought I had been lying to him for the past three months. Honestly, he was more upset about the state of my relationship than anything else. He really wanted my child to grow up in a two-parent household and for me to be happily married. The idea of me being a single mother at 21 was far from the life he envisioned for his little girl. We went back and forth in an argument until he finally said, "I'm coming to get that car." This would have been the third time he took my car as punishment. I tried to plead with him, explaining that I was six months pregnant and needed my car. I had nothing else and had to clear out my apartment that weekend. I begged him not to take it.

A few moments later, while I was lying in bed, I heard the beep of my car. When I looked out the window, I saw it speeding down the driveway. I quickly called my dad to ask if I could retrieve my belongings from the trunk. When I got outside, I was surprised to see my dad in his car ahead and his cousin in mine. Shocked, I asked his cousin, "What are you doing here? I thought you two were beefing." He replied, "We are, but your dad offered me $500 to help him get your car, so here I am." I said, "Okay, cool." That made me even angrier; my hormones were already out of control. While rummaging through the trunk, I spotted my custom skates. Grabbing them by the strings, I unleashed my frustration on my car, smashing the front and back windshields and denting the hood, roof, and doors. My dad was yelling from his car, "Pull off, pull off!" His cousin let me get my swings in before driving off, and my dad was furious. We did not speak again until after my son was born.

That weekend, even without a car, I still had to go to Las Vegas to clear out my apartment. My mom offered to take me, eager to hit the slot machines. However, as soon as we exited the freeway in Vegas, she hit the curb and broke the axle on her car. I should have taken that as a sign that things would go downhill. After a long day of traveling, dealing with a car accident, and waiting for a tow truck, I was exhausted. When we finally arrived at my apartment, I found nothing had been packed. No one was there, and I had to clear the place by the next day. My mom did not stick around to help; she headed to the nearest casino.

While I was in the apartment packing things up, Michelle showed up with her three children. The kids immediately ran to me, showering me affectionately and hugging my large belly. In stark contrast, Michelle came in ready for a fight. She told the kids not to speak to me, accused me of kicking them out, claimed I hated them, and said I did not care what happened to them. She was cursing and fussing but not doing anything, so I kept packing. The more I moved around, the angrier Michelle got. Amidst all the packing, I responded to her nonsense, matching her energy while never stopping the packing. Just in time, Amber walked in as Michelle reached for the scissors on the counter and attempted to cut me.

I had not seen or spoken to Amber since our big blowout, and I was unaware she had moved into my apartment with Michelle while I was in California. As Amber held Michelle back, she was telling her that I was not worth it, calling me all sorts of names and warning me that once I had my baby, she would deal with me—my day was coming. While all this was happening, I dragged trash bags out of the bedroom. Amber shouted at me not to touch her stuff. I replied that she was not supposed to be there, and everything needed to go, so I kept pulling out the bags. Suddenly, Amber grabbed one of her high heels and started hitting me on the back and the back of my head. I turned around and fought back; I could not understand why she would even try me. Just then, Michelle jumped in, and now both my sisters were attacking me while I was six months pregnant. Somehow, Amber ended up on the floor while Michelle had me in a chokehold, and my only option was to bite a chunk out of Michelle's arm for her to let me go.

The kids were crying, and there was blood everywhere. I was hyperventilating, terrified that they might have harmed my baby. I called 911, and they took the kids and left. While waiting for the paramedics, I had to call the casino to reach my mother since she did not have a cell phone. She did not come immediately; it took her a few hours because she said her machine was hot and she did not want to leave it. When she finally arrived, she was more upset about the police being involved than about how out of line Michelle and Amber had been. The next day, while I was away from the apartment, some neighbors saw Michelle and Amber retrieving their things from the dumpster and called the police, knowing what had happened the night before. When the officers arrived, Amber reportedly jumped over a wall to escape, while Michelle was caught on the spot. Michelle was arrested, and Amber had a warrant for her arrest.

After emptying my apartment, I returned to California to finish my pregnancy and spend my first year as a mother, not setting foot back in Vegas until New Year's Eve 2010. This time, my return to Vegas showed me that everything that I had gone through before was nothing compared to what lay ahead. The next few years of my life is truly a story to tell. I was faced with more lies, more deceit and betrayal to the point I tried to end it all.

Acknowledgements

With only half the story told, I would like to acknowledge those who saw me through the first half.

Nikki Reddix, the sister I got to choose. You have been an unwavering presence in my life. You have silently supported me at my lowest, continued to be there no matter the distance and the loudest in my success. You were a hard shell to crack but I thank you for giving in. I needed you without even realizing. I needed your friendship, your honesty, your loyalty, the laughs, the cries and everything in between. I love you beyond words and will forever cherish our sisterhood.

Lisa Hampton, my earthly angel. You have come to my rescue more times than I can remember. When I had nothing or no one, you were there for me. With no gain for yourself, you always ensured that I was okay. It didn't matter that we weren't related by blood; you embraced me as one of your own. Thank you for seeing me, seeing the potential in me, taking me in and supporting me. As for the rest of the family, you all know the place you hold in my heart; We are family forever.

In addition to those above I would also like to acknowledge the support system I had on the backend while writing this book. I was an emotional wreck, but my girls got me through.

Kisha Ryder, your words provided the inspiration for this book's title. One day, you asked me if I was aware of the Bible verse Psalm 119:71. I wasn't familiar with it, but you took the time to explain it to me, and we discussed affliction. After our conversation, I realized that my struggles had meaning and that my life had a purpose. Thank you for being there at just the right moment with exactly the right words. Also, thank you for being here every step of the way. You have been my second pair of eyes, my visual expert, and biggest support through this entire journey. I appreciate you a ton.

Kadijah and Jacque-O, I want to express my heartfelt gratitude for your unwavering support throughout this journey. I've shared my tears with you, talked your ears off, and even had you both beta-read my work. Your love and encouragement have meant the world to me. Some chapters were tough to navigate, but I always knew that if I reached out with even the slightest lump in my throat or a tear in my eye, you'd be there ready to listen. I'm incredibly grateful for both of you times a milli!

Lastly, I would like to acknowledge my family. My aim is to share my own story, not to recount yours. Through our experiences together, I have learned valuable lessons and grown stronger in the process. I hold no ill will towards anyone and have chosen to forgive all for everything that has transpired. Thank you for being a part of my journey. I love you all.

About the Author

Kori Moryn, a first-time author, shares her deeply personal journey in her debut autobiography, offering readers an intimate glimpse into her life experiences and the lessons she's learned along the way.

Based in vibrant Atlanta, GA, Kori balances her professional career in Information Technology, where she leverages her degree in Data Networking and Security, with her passion for creativity and self-expression. A true lover of fashion and photography, Kori finds joy in capturing beautiful moments and expressing her unique style.

Outside of her professional and creative pursuits, Kori cherishes her role as a mother to her beloved son. Her favorite moments are spent cooking delicious meals, exploring new destinations, and creating unforgettable memories with him.

Through her writing, Kori hopes to inspire others to embrace their stories, face challenges with resilience, and find beauty in every chapter of life.